CRICKET

·ON OLD PICTURE POSTCARDS·

Grenville Jennings

Yorkshire County Cricket Team 1923. Published by Fielding, Leeds.

Designed and Published by
Reflections of a Bygone Age
Keyworth, Nottingham.

Printed by Adlard Print and Typesetting Services,
Ruddington, Notts.

© **Grenville Jennings, June 1985.**

ISBN 0 946245 08 8

By the same author:
Nottingham and South Notts on old postcards

THE AUTHOR

Grenville Jennings was born in Nottingham and educated at High
Pavement Grammar School in the mid-1950's. He is a director of
Sitir (U.K.) Ltd., an export/import company based near East
Midlands Airport, and has collected Picture Postcards, specialis-
ing in Cricket and Nottingham cards, since 1977. He and his wife
Liz travel the country searching for these elusive mementoes of
the past to add to their already considerable collection.

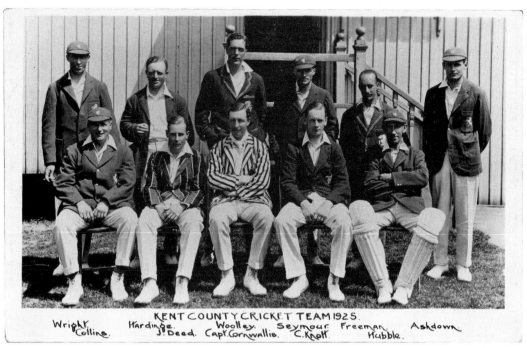

Kent County Cricket Team 1925. Postcard published by H.H. Camburn, Tunbridge Wells.

Contents

Overleaf: sales list of postcards published by E. Hawkins and Company of Brighton about 1909.

E. Hawkins and Company,

Photographers Royal & Cricket Specialists,

32, PRESTON STREET, BRIGHTON

(LATE OF 108, KING'S ROAD). ESTABLISHED 1847.

Celebrated First Class County Cricket Elevens, Australians, Philadelphians, South Africans, &c., &c., also Single Portraits of nearly every Cricketer of note.

E. HAWKINS & CO. have the Largest Collection of Cricket Photos in the Kingdom, having made it their Special Study since 1884. They receive Testimonials from all parts of the World.

THE FOLLOWING IS A SUPPLEMENT TO EARLIER LISTS—

DERBY.
E. M. ASHCROFT
WRIGHT, J.
F. C. HUNTER
L. G. WRIGHT
WARREN
HUMPHRIES, J.
CADMAN
MALTBY
MORTON
BESTWICK
NEEDHAM
R. B. RICKMAN
COOPER
BRACEY
SLATER
C. A. OLLIVIERRE
CARLIN
A. E. LAWTON
J. OLIVER
J. CHAPMAN

ESSEX.
F. L. FANE
C. McGAHEY
G. TOSSETTI
P. PERRIN
Rev. F. H. GILLINGHAM
J. W. H. T. DOUGLAS
R. P. KEIGWIN
C. J. KORTWRIGHT
A. P. LUCAS
BUCKENHAM
RUSSELL
SEWELL
CARPENTER
REEVES
OWEN
YOUNG
MEAD
BENHAM
FREEMAN, E. J.
TREMLIN
W. F. O. FAVIELL
D. C. ROBINSON
T. G. GRINTER
FREEMAN (J.)
M. G. SALTER

G. L. JESSOP
W. G. GRACE
S. A. P. KITCAT
W. S. A. BROWN
F. E. THOMAS
R. T. GODSELL
B. BARNETT
L. D. BROWNLEE
C. O. H. SEWELL
CAPT. CHAMPAIN
C. L. TOWNSEND
BOARD
WRATHALL
SPRY
DENNETT
HUGGINS
LANGDON
HALE
MILLS
W. H. NAISH
P. H. FORD
F. B. ROBERTS
J. N. WILLIAMS
CAPT. A. H. DU BOULAY
A. W. ROBERTS
G. W. HOLLOWAY
D. L. PRIESTLEY
WINSTONE
PARKER
DIPPER

GLO'STER.

HAMPSHIRE.
MAJOR POORE
A. J. L. HILL
D. M. EVANS
H. HESKETH-PRITCHARD
F. H. BACON
L. WALKER
D. A. STEELE
E. M. SPROT
CAPT. E. G. WYNYARD
REV. W. V. JEPHSON
HAYTER
LLEWELLYN
BALDWIN
STONE
WEBB
LANGFORD
BOWELL
C. ROBSON
SOAR
H. W. PERSSE
BADCOCK
MEAD
NEWMAN
A. C. JOHNSON
CAPT. N. W. WHITE
H. C. McDONELL
C. B. FRY
A. J. EVANS
REMNANT
BROWN
KENNEDY

KENT.
C. H. B. MARSHAM
E. W. DILLON
C. J. BURNUP
J. R. MASON
J. P. DAY
S. H. DAY
P. C. BAKER
R. N. R. BLAKER
FIELDER
FAIRSERVICE
SEYMOUR, J.
HEARNE, A.
HUMPHREYS, E.
BLYTHE
HUISH
HARDINGE
K. L. HUTCHINGS
BRADLEY

KENT.
MARTIN
WOOLLEY
HUBBLE
C. S. HURST
PRESTON

LANCASHIRE.
A. C. MacLAREN
R. H. SPOONER
H. G. GARNETT
W. FINDLAY
A. G. STEELE
A. H. HORNBY
L. O. S. POIDEVIN
W. BREARLEY
KERMODE
HEAP
TYLDESLEY
SHARP
CUTTELL
HALLOWS
RADCLIFFE
WORSLEY
HUDDLESTON
DEAN
GREGSON
MAKEPEACE
HARRY
H. D. STANNING
COOK
A. HARTLEY
A. F. SPOONER
K. G. MacLEOD
WHITEHEAD
PHILLIPS
BARNES, S. F.

LEICESTER.
C. E. DE TRAFFORD
V. F. S. CRAWFORD
R. T. CRAWFORD
C. J. B. WOOD
W. W. ODELL
A. E. DAVIS
KNIGHT
KING
WHITEHEAD
GILL
WHITESIDE
ALLSOPP
JAYES
COE
Sir A. HAZLERIGG
J. SHIELDS
J. S. CURTIS
ASTILL
SHIPMAN

MIDDLESEX.
G. MacGREGOR
P. F. WARNER
B. J. T. BOSANQUET
G. W. BELDAM
C. PALMER
W. P. ROBERTSON
R. E. MORE
C. M. WELLS
J. DOUGLAS
H. C. PILKINGTON
L. J. MOON
R. N. DOUGLAS
E. A. BELDAM
J. S. WELLS
A. R. LITTELJOHN
M. W. PAYNE
TROTT
MIGNON
HEARNE, J. T.
RAWLINS
TARRANT
C. P. FOLEY
C. V. BAKER
C. B. W. MAGNAY
W. P. HARRISON
E. S. LITTELJOHN
MURRELL
C. C. PAGE
L. G. COLBECK
J. HOUSTEAD
V. O'CONNOR
G. L. HEBDEN
HENDREN
HEARNE (J. W.)

NORTHAMPTON.
C. J. T. POOL
W. H. KINGSTON
H. E. KINGSTON
R. F. KNIGHT
R. C. SMITH
E. M. CROSSE
T. HORTON
EAST
COX
THOMPSON
BUSWELL
WELLS
G. A. T. VIALS
L. T. DRIFFIELD
A. R. THOMPSON

NOTTINGHAM.
A. O. JONES
C. R. MORRIS
R. E. HEMINGWAY
W. SPEAK
J. A. DIXON
GUNN, W.
GUNN, G.
GUNN, J.
IREMONGER
ANTHONY
OATES
DAY, J. W.
WASS
HARDSTAFF
HALLAM
PENNINGTON
PAYTON
JAMES
ALLETSON
G. T. BRANSTON
N. V. C. TURNER
RILEY

SOMERSET.
S. M. J. WOODS
L. C. H. PALAIRET
H. MARTYN
P. R. JOHNSON
H. S. POYNTZ
F. M. LEE
C. E. BROWN
F. A. PHILLIPS
LEWIS
BRAUND
NORTH
ROBSON
CRANFIELD
SELLICK
C. E. DUNLOP
BAILEY
W. G. BURROUGH
E. S. GOODLAND
J. DANIELL
CHIDGEY
WHITTLE

SURREY.
LORD DALMENY
E. M. DOWSON
J. E. RAPHAEL
H. D. G. LEVESON-GOWER
N. A. KNOX
MOULDER
STRUDWICK
HAYWARD
HOLLAND
NICE
SMITH, W. C.
DAVIS, W.
LOCKWOOD
STEDMAN
BAKER
GOODER
RICHARDSON
HOBBS
LEES
HAYES
I. V. HARPER
D. L. A. JEPHSON
J. N. CRAWFORD
RUSHBY
GOATLEY
MARSHAL
P. R. MAY
HITCH
BLACKLIDGE
PLATT
DUCAT

SUSSEX.
K. S. RANJITSINHJI
C. L. A. SMITH
G. BRANN
C. H. M. EBDEN
W. NEWHAM
K. O. GOLDIE
R. A. YOUNG
H. J. HEYGATE
P. H. LATHAM
H. P. CHAPLIN
BUTT
TATE
KILLICK
VINE
BLAND
LEACH
DWYER
COX
MARLOW
RELF, A.
CORDINGLEY
SEYMOUR
RELF, R.
H. L. SIMMS
J. W. W. NASON
VINCETT
C. E. LUCAS
J. C. BARLEY
CAPT. A. C. G. LUTHER
G. S. WHITFELD
J. V. YOUNG
W. H. RAMSBOTHAM
P. CARTWRIGHT
R. B. HEYGATE
RELF

WARWICK.
J. F. BYRNE
T. S. FISHWICK
F. R. LOVEITT
BAKER, C. S.
MOORHOUSE
FIELD
SANTALL
QUAIFE, W. G.
CHARLESWORTH
LILLEY
HARGREAVES
KINNEIR
WELDRICK
A. C. S. GLOVER
H. J. GOODWIN
F. G. STEPHENS
T. A. HILDITCH

WORCESTER.
R. E. FOSTER
H. K. FOSTER
W. L. FOSTER
G. N. FOSTER
G. H. SIMPSON-HAYWARD
A. W. ISAAC
Mr. BROMLEY-MARTIN
ARNOLD
BURROWS
PEARSON
GAUKRODGER
BOWLEY
AINLEY
KEENE
WILSON, G. A.
CUFFE
WHELDON
BIRD
W. E. C. HUTCHINGS
W. B. BURNS
HUNT
TURNER
BALE

YORKSHIRE.
LORD HAWKE
HON. F. S. JACKSON
E. SMITH
F. MITCHELL
H. WILKINSON
WHITEHEAD
HAIGH
HUNTER
HIRST
DENTON
GRIMSHAW
MYERS
RHODES
TUNNICLIFFE
WASHINGTON
DOLPHIN
RINGROSE
WILKINSON, W. H.
ROTHERY
T. L. TAYLOR
BATES
NEWSTEAD
DEYES
HARDISTY
WATSON
DRAKE
WILSON
WHITEHEAD, R. (trainer)

CAMBRIDGE.
F. B. WILSON
K R. B. FRY
C. H. EYRE
J. F. MARSH
J. G. HIRSCHE
E. W. MANN
G. M. BUCKSTON
F. R. ROBERTS
G. G. NAPIER
F. J. V. HOPLEY
H. MAINPRICE
A. MORCOM
J. N. BUCHANAN
C. C. G. WRIGHT
F. H. MUGLESTON
M. H. C. DOLL
R. E. H. BAILEY
J. REUNERT
E. OLIVIER
HON. C. F. LYTTELTON
J. H. B. LOCKHART
N. C. TUFNELL
J. F. IRELAND
M. FALCON
D. C. COLLINS

OXFORD.
W. H. B. EVANS
K. M. CARLISLE
E. G. MARTIN
A. VON ERNSTHAUSEN
R. C. W. BURN
M. BONHAM-CARTER
G. B. KNOX
H. J. WYLD
R. SALE
P. LE COUTEUR
J. C. M. LOWE
C. V. L. HOOMAN
A. G. PAWSON
R. O. LAGDEN
E. C. HATFIELD
F. H. TURNER

AUSTRALIANS.
J. DARLING
M. A. NOBLE
C. HILL
W. W. ARMSTRONG
A. J. HOPKINS
A. LAVER
D. R. A. GEHRS
W. P. HOWELL
P. M. NEWLANDS
A. COTTER
V. TRUMPER
R. A. DUFF
J. D. KELLY
C. E. McLEOD
P. A. McALISTER
H. CARTER
R. HARTIGAN
W. CARKEEK
W. J. WHITTY
J. A. O'CONNOR
C. G. MACARTNEY
V. RANSFORD
W. BARDSLEY

SOUTH AFRICANS.
L. J. TANCRED
J. H. KOTZE
W. A. SHALDERS
G. C. WHITE
M. HATHORN
J. H. SINCLAIR
S. J. SNOOKE
E. A. HALLIWELL
R. O. WORFORD
R. O. SCHWARZ
S. D. SNOOKE
A. D. NOURSE
G. A. FAULKNER
A. E. VOGLER
P. W. SHERWELL
H. SMITH
Rev. C. W. ROBINSON
G. ALLSOP

UMPIRES.
T. MYCROFT
J. PHILLIPS
J. E. WEST
W. ATTEWELL
H. BALDWIN
WILLOUGHBY
W. FLOWERS
A. MILLWARD
R. G. BARLOW
A. E. CLAPP
A. J. ATFIELD

LAWN TENNIS.
RITCHIE, M. J. G.
HILLYARD, G. W.
HILLYARD, MRS.
HILLYARD, MRS. and MR.
WILDING
HILLYARD, MRS. and MISS
MEYER
MAHONEY, H. S. (late)
GRANT, W. C.
WRIGHT, J. C.
RISELEY, F. L.
RISELEY, A. H.
WILDING, A. F.
CHAMBERS, Mrs. LAMBERT
(nee Miss K. Douglas.)
THOMSON, MISS
STERRY, MRS.
SMITH, S. H.
LUARD, MRS. and MR.
LUARD, MRS.
(nee Miss C. M. Wilson.)
LANE, MISS and MR.
BOOTHBY, MISS
CASDAGLI, X.
GANZONI, F.
SQUIRES, MISS
LONGHURST, MISS
GREEN, MISS
WESTFALL, H. L.
GORE, A. W.
PINCKNEY, MISS
WILSON, MISS and MRS.
STERRY
HOUSELANDER, MRS.
PREBBLE, A. D.
RISELEY, A. H. and MR.
REYNOLDS
WINCH, MRS.
McNAIR, R. J.
BEAMISH, A. E.
BENTLEY, A. L.
MEYER, MISS (late)
STONHAM, MISS
HEMPSTED, MRS.
(nee Miss S. Brown.)
BOUCHER, MISS
STOKES, J. F.
STOKES, J. F., and H. M. READ
CRAWLEY, W. C.
TAYLOR, A. E. M.
RAMSEY, MISS
WALLIS MYER
DOUST, S. N.
POWELL, R. B.
TRIPP, MISS J.
TUCKEY, A. D.
TUCKEY, MRS.
(nee Miss Daniella)
ADAMS, MISS
STOKES, J. F., and POWELL, R. B.
CARSON, H. J.
GODFREE, L. A.
Snapshots of Sussex Tennis Tournament, Hove, Brighton.

TENNIS.
JAY GOULD
PUNCH FAIRS
PETER LATHAM
FERDINAND GARCIN, etc.
World's Championship, 1907, and 1908, including many Champions, past and present.
A. WHITE and E. GRAY
R. DICKENSON and F. COVEY
C. (PUNCH) FAIRS and E. JOHNSON
P. LATHAM and C. (PUNCH) FAIRS

CROQUET.
BEATON, MRS.
(nee Miss Gower.)
BEATON, R. C. J.
WILLIS, MR.
NICHOLLS, MISS
WOOD, MISS
CARPMAIL, MISS
COOTE, MISS
TALBOT, MRS.
SPARTALI, MISS
GATEHOUSE, MISS
CURRY, J. E.
HOLLAND, A. C.
DU CANE, C. H. C.
CORBALLY, C.
O'CALLAGHAN, C. L.
HORNE, MISS
MINTON, MR.
ACKROYD, MR.
BRIGSTOCK, MRS.
KENYON-STOW, GENL.
MARSDEN, MRS.
STEWART, MISS
IZARD, H. K.
WILLIS, MISS, B.
AVERAHY JONES, MISS
BARLOW, MISS N.
HASSARD, MRS.
WHITE, MRS. F. H.
GREGORY, MISS
SELBY DONALDSON, T. S. and GREGORY, MISS
HEREPATH, MRS.
CHRISTIE, MISS
CHERTER, MISS
Views of Southwick Croquet Ground (snapshot).
Views of late Duke of Cambridge presenting prizes.

Large Selection of BRIGHTON VIEWS.

CHURCHES, ETC.

Cabinet and Post Card size.

Cabinet Photographs, 1/- each, or 10/- per dozen, assorted. Large Groups, 3/6 each. Terms—Cash with Order.
IMMEDIATE ATTENTION GIVEN TO PRESS WORK. NO CONNECTION WITH ANY OTHER FIRM.

CRICKET ON OLD PICTURE POSTCARDS

INTRODUCTION

A dual Golden Age

The Golden Age of cricket is generally recognised as being the years between 1900 and 1914: it runs almost parallel with the birth in Great Britain of the Picture Postcard (1894) and the period between 1900 and 1918 known as the 'Golden Age of Postcards' when Europe's postal system was swamped by the mailing of millions of cards every year.

Cricket has continued to grip the attention of the nation, with radio and television coverage and the one-day competitions giving it a more broadly-based following, but the popularity of the Picture Postcard declined sharply after the Great War, as other forms of communication improved.

The doubling of the postage rate in 1918, the increased effectiveness of newspapers, the general post-war mood, and the spread of the telephone habit all contributed to the diminishing importance of the Postcard as a national institution.

Start of the Picture Postcard boom

Picture Postcards in Britain were not sanctioned by the Post Office until 1894, although they had been in common use on the continent from the 1870's. The early British cards were known as Court Cards (size 115 x 89mm), smaller than the continental size of 140 x 89mm, and the message had to be written on the same side of the picture, leaving the back for the stamp and address. This obviously inhibited the possibilities for illustrations, so when the Post Office permitted the use of the larger-size card (1899) and the 'divided back' (1902) where message and address occupied the same side, the publishers were able to exploit the postcard much more effectively, and a flood of cards on every imaginable subject was produced.

Postcard Popularity

Postcard collecting was a major hobby in the first decade of this century, with many thousands of families amassing vast numbers of postcards sent from all over Britain and (for those with wealthy connections) the continent. Specialist magazines catered for the craze, and publishers produced cards on all kinds of themes, with a varying quality of printing. But with the cards published after 1918 reduced in numbers, variety and interest, few collectors kept up the habit once the Great War had ended: it was a new era, with changed values and priorities. 'Golden Age' postcards lay neglected in their albums in attics for years, until a few enthusiasts in the 1950's ushered in a new-found appreciation for the beautiful old cards to a whole new generation. Their availability, though, remained confined to the shelves of occasional book and antique shops, and new-wave collectors didn't find it easy to build up collections. All that changed in the 1970's. A travelling exhibition organised by the Victoria and Albert Museum, the emergence of specialist dealers, magazines, catalogues and fairs had the effect of encouraging a host of new collectors and a consequent upsurge in prices. By now, Edwardian albums were flooding from the attics as the original owners, or their sons and daughters died. Once again, eighty years on, the hobby is thriving, and the beautiful postcard issues of the Edwardian era are lovingly collected.

Cricket Postcards

Cricket was well-represented on postcards during the early days, and became one of the few themes that can claim a continuity of production through the century. Publishers quickly recognised the demand for the subject and the cricketing heroes of the Edwardian era were soon available on the cardboard medium.

Unlike other hobbies, the early postcard served a dual purpose, not only allowing the public, of whom a considerable number would no doubt be small boys, to view their heroes at close range - bear in mind the lack of newspaper photography, but also to transmit to their friends the state of play in a particular match, arrange meetings, advise travel plans etc., all for ½d plus the cost of a card, ranging from 1d to 6d for a packet of 12.

MR A.C. McLAREN.

1. A.C, McLaren (Lancashire and England) on a postcard published by Foster of Brighton. The card was posted at Manchester in July 1905.

2. The Australian XI poised to take on the 1907-8 English tourists who were led by A.O. Jones. This series was dominated by the home side, which eventually ran out winners by four Tests to one. At times, though, it seemed closer than that! The postcard was published by the London-based Pictorial Postcard Company in their 'Empire' series.

Major national publishers - Raphael Tuck, Wrench, Millar and Lang and Valentine's - produced cards of teams and players, and the subject lent itself to a host of comic interpretations. Small local publishers, too, were involved in the subject; indeed, the major producer of cricket cards in Britain was E. Hawkins, of Brighton, who apparently specialised exclusively in them. Mockford, of Tonbridge, was another example of a prolific publisher, and real photographic postcards featuring the county personalities were available from shops and county grounds. The tradition continued after 1918, with the emphasis on team photographs - particularly of the touring sides - and examples of cricket postcards can be found throughout the post-second world war period, too. The popularity of the subject has ensured that plenty of early cards have survived for today's collectors.

Coverage and scarcity

In Edwardian times, certain counties and players appeared more frequently than others on postcards: Kent, Lancashire, Middlesex, Nottinghamshire, Surrey and Yorkshire - and certain players featured more prominently, too, for example Rhodes, Hirst, Fry and Ranjitsinji.

There is an abundance of cards currently available of these counties and players, but experience has shown over the past seven or eight years that cards of Derbyshire, Leicestershire, Gloucestershire, Hampshire, Northamptonshire, Warwickshire and Worcestershire players are most difficult to find, Essex and Sussex obtainable, but of course Glamorgan (not first-class until 1921) a non-starter.

My own interest in collecting cards developed from collecting cricket books published prior to 1939. Postcards of Nottinghamshire players of the 1920's were to hand, but it was not until 1976 that collecting cards became serious. A colleague at work sold me a small lot of local Nottingham cards which led to an investigation of where more could be obtained, in turn leading to purchase of cricket cards at the reasonable cost of 40p for black and white cards, 75p for coloured ones. Two or three years earlier these were being sold for 4p each!

Because cricket was a very well-documented sport on postcards, there is enough material to satisfy readers who would like to begin building their own collections. Pre-1914 cards are most common, with county team photos selling from £3-£5, individual players £2-£4, and touring sides £4 upwards. The best cards are the real photographic ones, the worst the printed examples of the type published by Gottschalk, Dreyfus and Davis in their 'Star' series. Local teams can rate anything from £1 upwards, though demand from collectors of a particular area, as well as cricket enthusiasts, can inflate prices. Postcards of cricket grounds may sell from 50p-£2, while comic cards rate £1-£5, depending on the artist. Post-1919 material is in fact less common, with certain exceptions: the Australian tourists of 1921 and 1926 were featured comprehensively on cards. Scarcity of postcards of this era can in fact mean that you will have to pay more than for Edwardian items.

Signed examples will always command a premium.

Quoting prices is always a risky business, for they are apt to change, sometimes quickly, but it is safe to assume that it will be the rarest postcards that will rise in price most swiftly.

One problem with collecting cricket postcards is that most of the publishing records were either destroyed in one of the two World Wars, or lost forever when the firms closed down, thereby making original checklists of the various series and their contents unavailable. This, though, is what collecting is all about - plenty of research and satisfaction at the end. And there are exceptions to the lack of source material; we've reproduced, for instance, part of a sales list from Hawkins of Brighton on page 4. Contemporary collectors are gradually re-assembling the catalogues of cricketing postcards.

Aim of the book

The purpose of compiling these cards is to introduce to the uninitiated the pleasure of collecting cricket postcards. You will find household names of the day, International teams, cricket as an advertising medium and cricket as shown through the eyes of the comic artist. Hopefully, there is something for everyone, though the book is naturally aimed at the cricket enthusiast. The bulk of the cards are from the Golden Age period, there are a few of the 1920's and 1930's for comparison, and some show players whose careers spanned just a few seasons for whatever reason(s) prevailed at the time. Space, alas, permits only a cross-section of the cards available to choose from which will account for some apparent glaring omissions.

(continued on page 8)

3. A marvellous multi-view postcard of the England v Australia game at Trent Bridge during the 1926 tour. The game, unfortunately, was ruined by rain. This card - and a similar one commemorating the third Test at Leeds (featured on page 62) - was produced by Jack Webb of Nottingham.

4. Panoramic postcard view of the Old Trafford Grand Stand.

The Saffrons, Eastbourne

5. View from a relaxed part of the Saffrons at Eastbourne of a match in progress, and plenty of bowler hats in the foreground.

The Versatile Postcard

Unlike many other collectables, Picture Postcards are multi-faceted. Not only do they provide a picture of interest, but often a stamp, postmark and message, too. I prefer postally used ones - they're more 'complete'. Some people find the messages more interesting than the cards themselves! Finding postcards with a message referring to the picture, and a related postmark as well is really exciting. In addition, there is usually a publisher and series mentioned on the card, too.

Sources of supply

Lists of specialist Postcard dealers, auctions and fairs can be found in *Picture Postcard Monthly* and *Picture Postcard Annual* (see below)

Acknowledgements:

The following books have been consulted for statistical information.

Complete Who's Who of Test Cricketers (C. Martin-Jenkins); Orbis Publishing
Wisden
Who's Who of Cricketers (P. Bailey, P. Thorn, P. Wynne-Thomas); Guild Publishing - *from which most of the career records cited in this work have been taken.*

I should also like to thank

Geoffrey Copinger, for the Hawkins of Brighton sales list
Gordon Phillips, for the loan of illustrations 5, 234, 235 and 236.
Brian Lund, for the loan of illustrations 1, 4, 96, 115-138, 220-223, and those on the back cover.

Grenville Jennings, West Bridgford, June 1985.

Useful postcard reading for the beginner:

IPM Postcard Catalogue *(International Postcard Market, Carrick Mill House, Ponsanooth, Truro, Cornwall).*
RF Postcard Catalogue *(RF Postcards, 17 Hilary Crescent, Rayleigh, Essex).*
Stanley Gibbons Postcard Catalogue *(Stanley Gibbons, 399 Strand, London).*
Postcard Collecting - a beginners' guide *(Reflections of a Bygone Age, 15 Debdale Lane, Keyworth, Nottingham).*
Collecting Postcards 1894-1914 - Valerie Monahan and Wiliam Duval *(Longman)*
Picture Postcard Monthly *(Reflections of a Bygone Age).*
Picture Postcard Annual *(Reflections of a Bygone Age).*

6. Jack Hobbs (1882-1963), Surrey and England. Made his debut for Surrey in 1905 and went on to open the innings for his county and for England until 1934, scoring 61,760 runs (including 199 centuries). The postcard - note incorrection caption! - was published by Millar and Lang in their 'National Series', no. 773.

7. Kumar S. Ranjitsinghji, Sussex and England. A card portraying Ranji from the famous 'Vanity Fair' series published by Raphael Tuck and Sons, no. 1548.

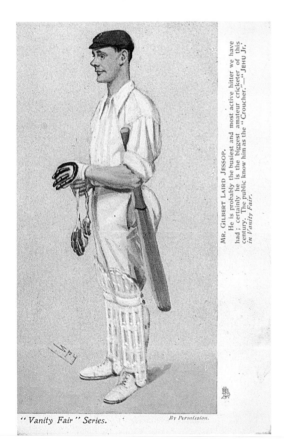

8. Gilbert L. Jessop, Gloucestershire and England. Another card in the Tuck 'Vanity Fair' series. This set of six is quite difficult to find.

9. John Tunnicliffe (1866-1948), Yorkshire. In a career spanning seventeen seasons, from 1891 to 1907, 'Long' John Tunnicliffe helped Yorkshire to seven County Championships, scoring a thousand runs in a season thirteen times and taking in excess of 500 catches, mostly at short slip. The postcard was published by Valentine's of Dundee.

10. W. Bestwick (1875-1938), Derbyshire and Glamorgan. In a career from 1898-1925, Beswick took 1,462 wickets, with his best performance 10-40 for Derbyshire against Glamorgan in 1921. Card published by E. Foster of Brighton.

11. W. Chatterton (1861-1913), Derbyshire and England. "In the box" postcard Series no. 1386 by F. Hartmann. Chatterton played just once for his country - against South Africa in 1891-2.

12. Claude P. Buckenham (1876-1937), Essex and England. In 258 appearances for Essex he captured 934 wickets at an average of 26.36, and played in four tests against South Africa in 1909-10. E. Hawkins of Brighton published the card.

13. Charles P. McGahey (1871-1935), Essex and England. Hartmann series no. 1666. C.P. McGahey scored more than 20,000 runs between 1894 and 1923, including 31 centuries, and twice appeared in a test against Australia in 1901.

14. Harry Wrathall (1869-1944), Gloucestershire. Played from 1894-1907, and scored in all 11,023 runs. During this period he served under probably the two most famous players in the history of the game, W.G. Grace and G.L. Jessop. Postcard publisher unknown.

15. Gilbert L. Jessop (1874-1955), Cambridge, Gloucestershire and England. Although he appeared in 18 Test matches, Jessop never really produced his county cricket form there.
He was without doubt the most famous hitter of all time, a fast bowler, and an exceptional fielder. He scored 26,698 runs in his career, and took 873 wickets from 1894-1914. Card published by F. Hartmann, no. 1662.

G. Llewellyn.

The Wrench Series No. 1753.

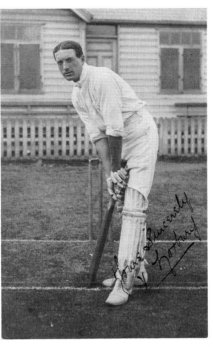

16. Charles B. Llewellyn (1876-1964). A Wrench postcard (no. 1753) featuring the Hampshire, Natal and South Africa cricketer. In his career, from 1894 to 1912, this fine all-rounder scored 11,425 runs (including 18 centuries), and took 1013 wickets, appearing in 15 Tests for South Africa.

17. Victor Norbury (1887-1972), Hampshire, Northumberland and Lancashire. Played spasmodically for the former in 1905-6 and the latter in 1919-22. The postcard has no publisher's or photographer's name.

18. Jack A. Newman (1884-1973), Hampshire. Another anonymously-produced card of a cricketer who scored over 15,000 runs and took more than 2,000 wickets in a career stretching from 1906 to 1930. J.A. Newman played 507 times for Hampshire, and in 1927 had match figures of 16-88 against Somerset at Weston-super-Mare.

J. HUMPHRIES A. WARREN W. BESTWICK G. CURGENVEN L. G. WRIGHT S. NEEDHAM
W. STORER C. A. OLLIVIERRE S. M. ASHCROFT (CAPTAIN) S. CADMAN H. F. WRIGHT
DERBYSHIRE. COPYRIGHT

19. Derbyshire C.C. 1904 on a postcard published by Gottschalk, Dreyfus and Davis in the 'Star' series. These cards were produced in book form, each one having a perforated edge so the cards could be torn off as required. Though very popular, they were probably the poorest of all cricket postcards.

20. Essex C.C., about 1913. Published by John Hart of Leytonstone, this card shows an Essex team captained by J.W.H.T. Douglas and including (seated far left) the Rev. F.H. Gillingham, who between 1903 and 1928 scored over 9,000 runs.

21. Gloucestershire XI, 1903. Published by the Rotary Photo Co. in their photographic series, this postcard is autographed on the reverse by Wrathall, Board, Sellick, Spry, Dennett, Huggins and Langdon.

22. Gloucester XI in 1906, when they finished ninth in the county table - Kent were Champions. There is no indication of the publisher or photographer but the card was postally used from Cheltenham on 11th July 1907. We learn from 'Wilt' that he went to Gloster on Saturday night - *"it is about 9 miles by train - nice and lively too."*

23. James Stone (1876-1942), Hampshire and Glamorgan. In a career for Hampshire lasting from 1900 to 1914, Stone not only kept wicket but proved at times a more than useful batsman, scoring in all 9,167 runs. After the Great War, he appeared on several occasions for Glamorgan, totalling another 1,047. Card published anonymously.

S 11393   KENT CRICKETERS- D. W. JENNINGS.

24. D.W. Jennings (1889-1917), Kent. A W.H. Smith "Kingsway" series postcard of a young man who died in August 1918 in Tunbridge Wells hospital after suffering from shell shock and gas, encountered while serving with the Kent Fortress Engineers. He played infrequently for Kent from 1909 to 1914 due to the county's formidable batting line-up, but he did score three hundreds.

LLEWLLYN   WEBB   LANGFORD   BALDWIN   BOWELL   HAYTER
STONE   J. H. BACON   MAJOR POORE (CAPTAIN)   D. A. STEELE   D. M. EVANS
PHOTO HAWKINS, BRIGHTON   HAMPSHIRE.   COPYRIGHT

25. Hampshire C.C., 1904. Another card in the 'Star' series by Gottschalk, Dreyfus and Davis. It includes Major R.M. Poore, the county's captain, who played when his army duties permitted on and off between 1899 and 1906, achieving a highest score of 304 against Somerset in 1899.

26. Kent C.C., 1906. A card by J.F. Mockford of Tonbridge, who produced many fine postcards of the players and teams in the early and mid-1900's. 1906 was a Championship-winning year for Kent.

Humphreys,   Woolley,   Huish,   Seymour,   Hearne,
Fielder,   Hubble,   R. N. R. Blaker,   C. H. B. Marsham, Capt.,   J. R. Mason,   Fairservice,   K. L. Hutchings.
Photo, J. F. Mockford]   KENT CRICKET TEAM, 1906.   [Tonbridge.

COTTELL (W.)   HALLOWS (J.)   KERMODE (A.)   A.C. MACLAREN   (RANSON J.)   TYLDESLEY (J.T.)
H.G. GARNETT.   L.O.S POIDEVIN   R.H. SPOONER   W. BREARLEY   SHARP...

27. Lancashire in 1905 when they finished runners-up in the County Championship to Yorkshire. Card published by Delittle, Fenwick and Co. of York.

28. Kent, 1903, featured in the Rotary Photographic series. Middlesex were Champions that season, while Kent finished joint eighth with Essex.

29. C.J. Burnup (1875-1960), Cambridge and Kent, on a Mockford of Tonbridge card. In a career lasting from 1896 to 1907 (he was captain of Kent in 1903), scored 13,614 runs with 26 centuries.

30. Frank Woolley (1887-1978), Kent and England. A young Woolley portrayed here by Mockford. Between 1906 and 1938 he scored 58,959 runs with a highest score of 305 not out, and appeared 64 times for England.

31. Arthur O. Jones (1872-1914), Cambridgeshire, Nottinghamshire and England. A brilliant opening bat, astute captain, and exceptional fielder, Jones scored 22,935 runs between 1892 and 1914. For good measure, he took 577 catches and 333 wickets, leading Nottinghamshire to their only Championship during the 'Golden Age', in 1907. Arthur Jones appeared in 12 Test matches, and was captain on the Australian Tour of 1907-8. Postcard by Millar and Lang in their 'National' series, no. 773.

32. Johnny T. Tyldesley (1873-1930), Lancashire and England. Appearing in 31 Tests for England, this fine right-handed batsman played for Lancashire from 1895 to 1923, scoring 37,897 runs, including 86 centuries. Considered to be a brilliant bat and extremely fast outfielder, he was the elder brother of Ernest Tyldesley, another fine runmaker. 'National' series no. 773.

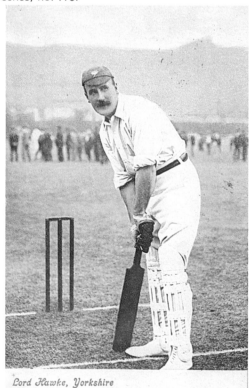

33. Hon. M.B. Hawke (1860-1930), Cambridge, Yorkshire and England. Lord Hawke, as he became in 1887, played for Yorkshire from 1881-1911 (captain 1883-1910). During this time, he scored 16,479 runs. He played for England on five occasions, but with little success.

34. George J. Thompson (1877-1943), Northamptonshire and England. G.J. Thompson is alleged to be the man who bowled his county into first-class cricket in 1905, after sterling feats against minor counties. A fast-medium bowler and competent bat, he took 1,591 wickets and scored 12,018 runs in first-class games from 1897 to 1922, and played in six Tests. 'National' series no. 828.

35. Kent, Champion County in 1909. Postcard published by local company Young and Cooper of Maidstone.

36. F.H. Knott (1891-1972), Oxford and Kent. He first appeared for Kent in 1910 when captain of Tonbridge School, scoring 114 against Worcestershire late in the season. Though he eventually captained Oxford to a win over Cambridge in 1914, he never fulfilled his schoolboy brilliance, and consequently played in very few first-class matches. Card published anonymously.

37. Arthur Mold (1865-1921), Lancashire and England. An extremely fast bowler whose career sadly ended in 1901 after he was no-balled for throwing. He played from 1889, taking 1,673 wickets at an average of 15.54, and appearing in three Tests against Australia in 1893. The postcard is no. 1381 in F. Hartmann's series.

38. Jack Sharp (1878-1938), Lancashire and England. A fine all-round sportsman who scored over 20,000 runs (with 38 centuries) for his county, and played in three Tests. Sharp was also an accomplished footballer with Everton and England. The photo is by Foster of Brighton for W.H. Smith's 'Grosvenor' series.

-17-

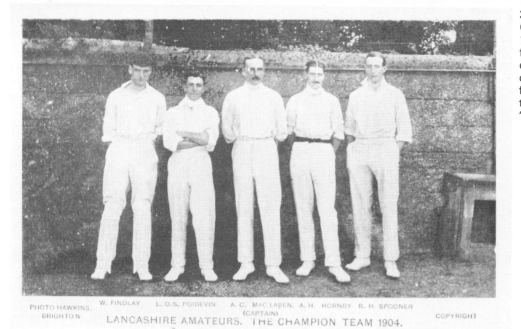

PHOTO HAWKINS. BRIGHTON   W. FINDLAY   L. O. S. POIDEVIN   A. C. MAC LAREN (CAPTAIN)   A. H. HORNBY   R. H. SPOONER   COPYRIGHT

LANCASHIRE AMATEURS. THE CHAMPION TEAM 1904.

39. The Lancashire Championship-winning team of 1904 portrayed in segregated form on this and the following card. The Amateurs, including captain Archie Maclaren, are featured on this postcard in Gottschalk, Dreyfus and Davis's 'Star' series.

40. Lancashire Professionals 1904. Photo by Hawkins & Son, Brighton, for W.H. Smith's 'Grosvenor' series.

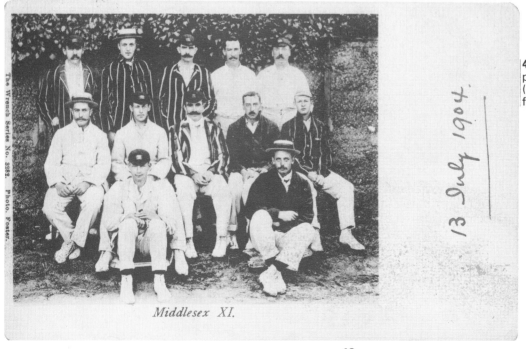

HEAP.   CUTTELL.   KERMODE.   TYLDESLEY.   HALLOWS.   SLADEN.   SHARP.   HAWKINS & SON BRIGHTON

LANCASHIRE CRICKET TEAM. (Professional.)

The Wrench Series No. 3282. Photo. Foster.

Middlesex XI.

41. Middlesex XI, 1904, on a postcard published by Wrench (no. 3282). The team finished fourth in the table that year.

42. Sydney F. Barnes (1873-1967), Warwickshire, Staffordshire, Lancashire and England. Unusual as it may seem, one of the greatest bowlers of all time played in less than ten seasons in first-class cricket, much preferring the Staffordshire leagues. S.F. Barnes played in 27 Tests, taking 189 wickets at an average of 16.43. Card published by Hawkins, Brighton.

43. Walter Brealey (1876-1937), Lancashire and England. A right-arm fast bowler who played between 1902 and 1921, during which time he took 844 wickets (average 19.31) and played 4 Tests, against Australia and South Africa. A Hawkins of Brighton postcard.

44. Arthur E. Knight (1872-1946) Leicestershire and England. A deeply religious man who played from 1895-1912 and scored 19,357 runs, A.E. Knight made 3 Test appearances. F. Hartmann published the card.

45. John H. King (1871-1946), Leicestershire and England. He was a fine all-rounder and in his 502 county appearances, between 1894 and 1925, scored over 20,000 runs and took 1,204 wickets. King made a single Test appearance in 1909 against Australia. Another Hawkins postcard.

46. Sir Pelham F. Warner (1873-1963), Oxford, Middlesex and England. 'Plum' Warner was born in Trinidad and played for Middlesex from 1894 to 1920. He was a fine batsman and scored 29,028 runs, with 60 centuries, and was a prolific writer on the game, being correspondent for the *Morning Post*. In 1937 he was knighted for services to cricket. A Hartmann card.

47. Albert E. Trott (1873-1914), Victoria, Middlesex, England, and Australia. A belligerent striker of the ball, who, after appearing in three Tests for Australia in the 1894-5 series, later played for Middlesex from 1898-1910, and also played twice for England against South Africa in 1898-9. Took his own life in August 1914. This postcard is in the Wrench series, no. 1754.

48. Bernard J.T. Bosanquet (1877-1936), Oxford, Middlesex and England. This Hartmann-published card features the father of the famous late T.V. personality 'Reggie' Bosanquet. In his own right, the elder Bosanquet was famous for discovering the "googly". A fine cricketer, he scored 21 first-class centuries and played seven times for his country.

49. Gregor MacGregor (1869-1919), Cambridge, Middlesex and England. An extremely skilful wicket-keeper who first played for England (against Australia) in 1890. He was renowned for his fearless practice of standing up close to the wicket when keeping to the fastest bowlers of his day, and was a more than useful batsman. He aggregated 559 dismissals between 1888 and 1907, and appeared in eight Tests. One of the 'Star' series of cards.

50. William Gunn (1858-1921), Nottinghamshire and England. A right-handed batsman of extreme elegance who made his debut for Notts in 1880, and was until 1904 a stalwart of the team, scoring over 25,000 runs, including 48 centuries. Gunn played in 11 Tests, and as a professional footballer with Notts County earned two international caps. Card published by Giesen Brothers and printed in Berlin.

51. Leicestershire XI, 1905, on a postcard by Foster of Brighton. Led by C. De Taafford, Leicester finished in fifth position in the County Championship, at the time their best-ever performance. Their leading players were C.J.B. Wood, who scored 1,567 runs, A.E. Knight with 1,085 runs, and bowlers Odell (76 wickets) and Jayes (95).

52. Nottinghamshire, 1911. Led by A.O. Jones, Notts finished eighth in the Championship, and it was in this season that Ted Alletson, seated to the immediate left of his captain, scored his whirl-wind 189 in 90 minutes against Sussex at Hove. This card (by E. Hawkins and Co., Brighton) may have been produced during that game, as it was Hawkins' normal practice to photograph visiting players and teams on their visit to Sussex.

53. George Gunn (1879-1958), Nottinghamshire and England. Nephew of William Gunn, George became one of his county's finest opening batsmen, thriving on fast bowling. His eccentricities had the greatest bowlers of the day at their wits' end. Between 1902 and 1932, he scored 35,208 runs (with 62 centuries), in later years appearing with his son G.V. Gunn - both scored centuries against Warwickshire in 1931. George played in 13 Tests. Postcard by Gottschalk, Dreyfus and Davis in the 'Star' series.

54. Arthur Shrewsbury (1856-1903), Nottingham-shire and England. Alleged to be one of the greatest bad-wicket players of all time, and the most famous professional of his day, Shrewsbury played for Notts from 1875 to 1902, scoring 26,505 runs and appearing in 23 Tests. He committed suicide in 1903 when he mistakenly thought he had an incurable illness. Wrench series (no. 1750) postcard.

J. IREMONGER.

JOHN GUNN.

T. WASS.

55. Jimmy Iremonger (1876-1956), Nottinghamshire. A fine opening bat who scored 16,622 runs for Notts from 1897 to 1914, forming a splendid opening partnership with A.O. Jones. Brother of the famous "Albert" (goalkeeper with Notts County F.C.), Jimmy also played football - at left back - for Nottingham Forest, and appeared three times for England in that position. Wrench series card, no. 2939.

56. John R. Gunn (1876-1963), Nottinghamshire and England. Brother of George, this fine all-rounder played for Notts from 1896 to 1925, scoring 24,557 runs and taking 1,242 wickets. In six Tests for his country he took 18 wickets, but did nothing with the bat. After 1925, he became associated with the great Nottinghamshire benefactor Sir Julien Cahn, appearing many times for his team. Card published in the Wrench series, no. 1691.

57. T.G. Wass (1873-1953), Nottinghamshire. 'Topsy' Wass formed a most formidable bowling partnership with A.W. Hallam. On many occasions they wheeled away unchanged through a complete innings. In the Championship win of 1907, Wass took 145 wickets, Hallam 153 - next highest wicket-taker was John Gunn with 25! Wass took 1,666 wickets between 1896 and 1920. 'Star' series card.

Somerset XI.

58. Somerset - probably the 1904 side, on a Wrench series card, no. 3279.

59. Surrey, about 1906, photographed by R. Scott and Company, Manchester. This is a typical example of how difficult it is to date some postcards. On the back row, third from left, is Marshall, who according to the records, did not begin playing until 1907. Two players away is Nice, whose career finished in 1905! Another card in my collection shows M.T. Jackson's photo in place of Marshal's. The most likely explanation is that old cards were re-touched for economy reasons to avoid total reprints. Note a young Jack Hobbs in the back row.

Photo by R. Scott & Co.,   **SURREY CRICKET CLUB.**   *Manchester.*
Strudwick.   Baker.   Marshall.   Holland.   Nice.   Hobbs.   J. N Crawford.
Hayes.   N. A. Knox.   Lord Dalmeny.   Hayward.   Lees.

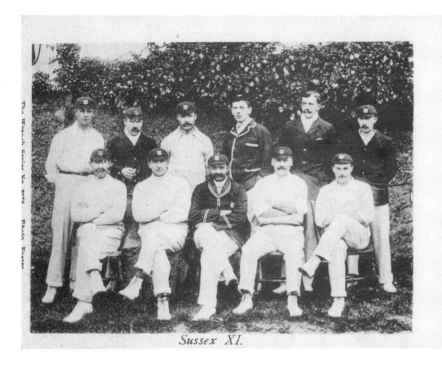

Sussex XI.

60. Sussex 1904, portrayed in the Wrench series, no. 3278. The great Ranjitsinji is seated in the middle of the front row, and to his left, his equally great companion, C.B. Fry.

A cricketing year

In 1906, the Surrey team pictured in illustration 59 finished third in the county championship, behind Yorkshire and the winners, Kent. Eighteen of their twenty-eight games were won, and four lost. *Wisden* rated the season a "brilliant success" for them. Hayward led the batting with a magnificent 3,246 runs at an average of 72.13, while Knox topped the bowling averages with 129 wickets at 19.00 each. Leading wicket-taker, though, was Walter Lees, with 154. It was his benefit season, and he was given the Yorkshire match, proceeds from which amounted to a handsome £2,120. Surrey won this game by nine wickets, and attendance over the three days was about 80,000.

Five *Wisden* Cricketers of the Year were J.N. Crawford (Surrey), who in 1906 became the youngest first-class cricketer to achieve the double, E.G. Hayes (Surrey), K.L. Hutchings (Kent), N.A. Knox (Surrey), and A. Fielder (Kent).

61. J. Daniels (1878-1963), Cambridge and Somerset. Captain of his county from 1919-26, this fearless fielder and hard-hitting batsman scored over ten thousand runs from 1898-1927. He was also an excellent rugby footballer and played for England, twice being captain. Card published by E. Hawkins & Co., Brighton.

MR. L. C. H. PALAIRET.

62. Lionel C.H. Palairet (1870-1933), Oxford, Somerset and England. A most elegant batsman who scored over 15,000 runs from 1891 to 1909, with a highest score of 292 against Hampshire in 1896. His career included two Tests against Australia in 1902. Wrench series card, no. 2935.

63. Len C. Braund (1875-1955), Surrey, Somerset and England. Braund was an outstanding all-round professional who, discarded by Surrey in 1898, established himself with Somerset as a top-class player in a career spanning 1899 to 1920. He scored 17,801 runs, and took 1,114 wickets and 545 catches. He played 23 times for England. Card by E. Hawkins of Brighton.

64. Henry Martyn (1877-1928), Oxford and Somerset. Acknowledged as one of the finest wicket-keepers of his day, Martyn played for his county from 1901 to 1908, though he never appeared in a Test, largely because Dick Lilley of Warwickshire was in his prime at the same time. Another Hawkins card.

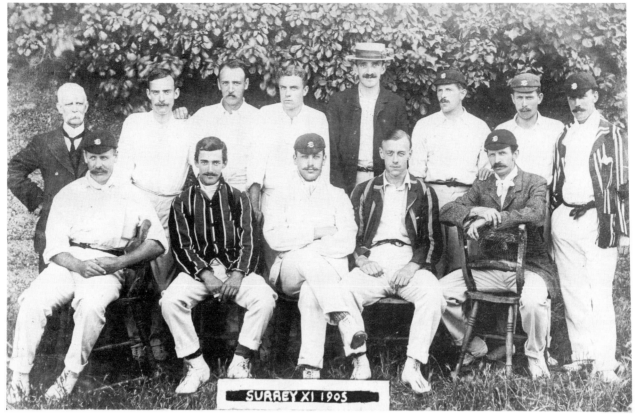

65. Surrey C.C., 1905, by Foster of Brighton. Led by Lord Dalmeny, Surrey rose from eleventh in 1904 to fifth in 1905, principally due to their bowlers. Walter Lees captured 169 wickets and Neville Knox 105.

66. Sir Henry D.G. Leverson-Gower (1873-1954), Oxford, Surrey and England. A small man, nicknamed 'Shrimp', who in a career from 1893 to 1931 scored over 7,000 runs and played in three Tests against South Africa in 1909-10. He later became President of Surrey and was knighted in 1953 for his services to cricket. A Hawkins of Brighton postcard.

67. W.H. "Billy" Lockwood (1868-1932), Nottinghamshire, Surrey and England. Due to an abundance of talent, he left Notts for Surrey in 1888, to play with distinction for that county until 1904. He was a great fast bowler and no mean bat, who overcame personal tragedy which led to loss of form and a drink problem from 1895-7. In all, he captured 1,376 wickets and scored over 10,000 runs, and played in 12 Tests. This postcard was published by the Rotary Photo Co., no. 3803.

68. William Brockwell (1865-1935), Surrey and England. The backbone of the strong Surrey team of the 1890's, Brockwell was an exceptional right-hand bat and a more than useful bowler. From 1886 to 1903, he scored 13,285 runs and took 553 wickets, though he never did justice to himself in the seven Tests in which he appeared. During his career, Brockwell was always well-turned out, and in his private life a man of many interests. Sadly, after retirement, he fell on hard times and died in relative poverty. Postcard by Giesen Bros. & Co.

Rushby.
Lees.   Hayes.   Holland.   Hobbs.   Smith.   Marshal.   Boyington (Scorer)
Lord Dalmeny.   H. D. G. Leveson-Gower.   J. N. Crawford.   Hayward.
Strudwick.   Baker.

Series 4041.   **Surrey, 1908.**   Davidson Brothers.

69. Surrey 1908, a real photographic card by Davidson Brothers, series no. 4041. Under Leverson-Gower, Surrey finished third in the Championship - won that year by Yorkshire.

70. Sussex XI 1903, by Rotary Photo Co., no. 3816. Sussex were second in the Championship in this season, with Ranjit-sinji and Fry in magnificent form, with 5 and 9 hundreds respectively. They finished first and second in the national averages.

RELF   G. BRANN.   TATE.   *SUSSEX XI.*   W. NEWHAM.   BUTT   COX
C. B. FRY.   VINE.   K. S. RANJITSINHJI (*CAPT*)   KILLICK.   BLAND.
1816. ROTARY PHOTO E.C.

71. Sussex 1905, published by Foster of Brighton in the year the county finished third in the Championship. C.B. Fry scored seven hundreds, and Cox, Killick and A.E. Relf each took over 100 wickets.

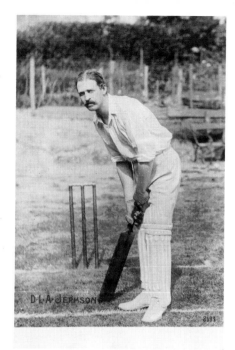

72. Digby Jephson (1871-1926), Cambridge and Surrey. Played for the county between 1894 and 1904, and was captain in 1901-2. He was a most useful hard-hitting batsman and a skilful 'lob' bowler, scoring 7,973 runs, and taking 297 wickets at an average of 25.10. Publisher of the postcard unknown.

73. C.L.A. Smith (1879-1949), Sussex. Played from 1898 to 1911, and took over the captaincy from C.B. Fry in 1906 when the latter was injured. Smith scored over 5,000 runs from Sussex, and was the player who caught Ted Alletson in 1911, ending the famous innings of 189 runs in 90 minutes. Card published by Foster of Brighton and postally used in September 1905.

74. Joe Vine (1875-1946), Sussex and England. Vine played for Sussex from 1896 to 1922, during which time he had many fine opening partnerships with C.B. Fry. In all, he scored 25,171 runs, averaging 29.94, and appeared in two Tests against Australia in 1911-12. A Hawkins of Brighton postcard.

75. K.S. Ranjitsinji (1872-1933), Cambridge, Sussex and England. This postcard, published by Giesen Brothers, shows H.H. Jam Sahib of Nawangar - Ranji, or 'Smith' as he was called at Cambridge. The legendary Indian prince who played for Sussex from 1895 to 1920 was acknowledged by the cricket fraternity as a genius. He scored 24,692 runs (72 centuries) in his career, playing 15 Tests for England.

76. Richard A. Young (1885-1968), Cambridge, Sussex and England. Played for Sussex from 1905 to 1925 when his duties as Maths teacher at Eton permitted. Young wore spectacles, unusual in his day for any sportsman, and represented England at both cricket and soccer. In all he scored 6,653 runs with eleven centuries. A Hawkins of Brighton postcard.

77. Sam Hargreave (1875-1929), Warwickshire. Hartmann series postcard no. 2913. Hargreave first played for the county in 1899, appearing regularly for the next ten seasons. He took 919 wickets, averaging 21.84.

W. G. QUAIFE.

Mr. F.R. Foster,
Captain of the Warwickshire
County Cricket Club.

78. E.J. 'Tiger' Smith (1886-1979), Warwickshire and England. First played for Warwickshire as understudy wicket-keeper to Dick Lilley in 1904, and remained as a player until 1930. Smith captured 877 victims, and played in 11 Tests for England. Another Hawkins postcard.

79. William G. Quaife (1872-1951), Sussex, Warwickshire and England. He originally joined Sussex with his elder brother Walter, but after one season went to Warwickshire in 1894. Though small, he was a most consistent run-gatherer, accumulating 36,012 up to 1928, and playing his last match at the age of 56. His career included seven Tests for England. No. 2932 in the Wrench series.

80. Frank R. Foster (1889-1958), Warwickshire and England. Led his county to their first Championship in 1911. A fine fast bowler and an aggressive striker of the ball, he featured in 11 Test matches for England. Sadly, his career was finished prematurely by a motorcycle accident. Published locally in Birmingham by Adams and Co.

81. R.D. Burrows (1871-1943), Worcestershire. Dick Burrows, when in form, was a genuine fast bowler - but could on occasions be very erratic. He played in the Worcester team for almost twenty years, during which time he took 894 wickets, averaging 26.40. Card published by Foster of Brighton.

82. Fred L. Bowley (1873-1943), Worcestershire. A more sound and consistent batsman it would be difficult to find. He joined Worcestershire in 1899 and played for a further 24 seasons, scoring 21,122 runs, averaging 29.62. Another Foster publication.

83. Fred Pearson (1880-1963), Worcestershire. Played as an all-round professional for the county from 1900-26, scoring 18,735 runs and taking 853 wickets. Six times he exceeded a thousand runs in a season, and in 1923 achieved the double. Postcard published by Foster of Brighton.

84. Edward G. Arnold (1876-1942), Worcestershire and England. This talented all-rounder played for Worcester from 1899 to 1913 and appeared in ten Tests, playing an important part (with his bowling) as a leading member of P.F. Warner's Ashes-winning team in Australia in 1903-4. In all he scored 15,853 runs and took 1069 wickets. No publisher indicated on the card.

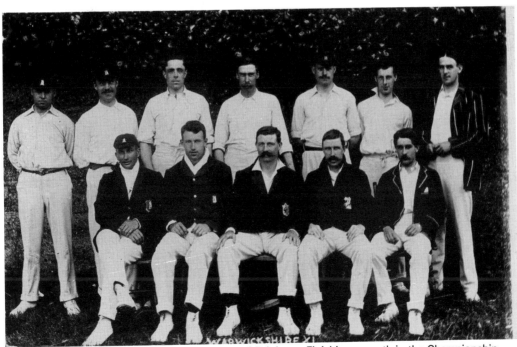

85. Warwickshire, 1905, on a card by Foster of Brighton. Finishing seventh in the Championship, the side, led by J.F. Byrne, did not win a match until the beginning of July. They must have been pleased with their final position!

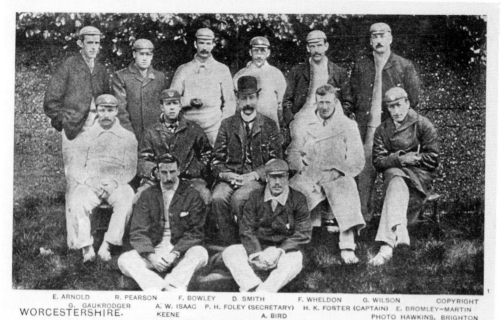

E. ARNOLD   R. PEARSON   F. BOWLEY   D. SMITH   F. WHELDON   G. WILSON   COPYRIGHT
G. GAUKRODGER   A. W. ISAAC   P. H. FOLEY (SECRETARY)   H. K. FOSTER (CAPTAIN)   E. BROMLEY—MARTIN
WORCESTERSHIRE.   KEENE   A. BIRD   PHOTO HAWKINS, BRIGHTON

86. Worcestershire, 1904, in the 'Star' series. This was the year that the county, captained by H.K. Foster, finished 13th in the Championship. The lack of success was possibly due to their not having the services of another of the famous family - R.E. Foster, the brilliant batsman.

87. Yorkshire, 1908, portrayed by Davidson Bros. (series no. 4107). Lord Hawke was still very much in command, ably supported by the bowling trio of Haigh, Hirst, and Rhodes, plus the ever-reliable batting of David Denton. At the time, some surprise was felt when Yorkshire won the Championship in that year, but George Hirst felt it was the fielding that got them through. A notable contribution that season came from the all-round cricket of Newstead (extreme left, back row).

Newstead.   Rothery.   J. Hoyland.   Denton.   Wilkinson W. H.   Bates
Hunter.   Hirst.   Lord Hawke.   Haigh.   Rhodes.
      Myers.   Grimshaw.

Series 4107.   **Yorkshire, 1908.**   Davidson Brothers

88. David Hunter (1860-1927), Yorkshire. Took over from his brother Joe, who had retired as Yorkshire wicket-keeper in 1888 due to ill-health. Up to 1909, Hunter dismissed 1,265 batsmen, helping the trio mentioned above, and earlier the legendary Bobby Peel. Card published by Hawkins of Brighton.

89. Wilfred Rhodes (1877-1973), Yorkshire and England. Truly a remarkable cricketer: a slow left-hand bowler of the highest standard, and a Test number eleven batsman with sufficient ability eventually to open for his country with Jack Hobbs. From 1898 to 1930, he scored 39,969 runs and took 4,204 wickets, averaging 16.71. Rhodes made 58 appearances for England. Card published by G.W. Richmond of Darlington.

W. RHODES.

-30-

90. George Hirst (1871-1954), Yorkshire and England. Like his contemporary, Rhodes, was one of the legends of Yorkshire cricket. He was the only player ever to achieve the feat of taking over 200 wickets and score two thousand runs in a season (1906). Hirst made his debut for Yorkshire in 1891, and up to 1929 scored 36,356 runs and took 2,742 wickets; he played in 24 Tests. Postcard by Giesen Bros.

91. Schofield Haigh (1871-1921), Yorkshire and England. From 1895 to 1913, Haigh was a member of the very powerful county team that won the Championship regularly. A right-arm medium-fast bowler who later became a good bat as his career record of 2,012 wickets and 11,715 runs would indicate. Made eleven appearances for England. Wrench series (no. 2940) postcard.

92. W.A.I. Washington (1879-1927), Yorkshire. Another Wrench card, no. 2943. A left-handed bat of unusual promise, he had to cut short his career after the 1902 season due to ill-health. From 1900-2, scored 1,384 runs at an average of 21.96.

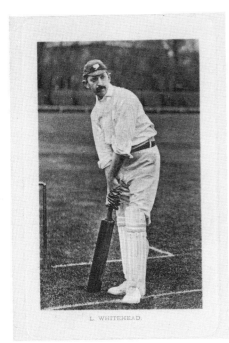

93. Lees Whitehead (1864-1913), Yorkshire. While not a regular member of the strong Yorkshire team of the 1890's, Whitehead was acknowledged as being a useful cricketer. He first appeared for the county in 1889, and played until 1904, scoring 2,433 runs and taking 109 wickets. He died of pneumonia in 1913. Wrench series, no. 4687.

94. John Newstead (1877-1952), Yorkshire. In 1908 Newstead was nominated as one of Wisden's five cricketers of the year, due to his fine bowling which assited Yorkshire's Championship win. He first played in 1903, and on finishing his career ten years later had taken 310 wickets at an average of 19.18. The postcard is by Hawkins, Brighton.

95. Jack T. Brown (1869-1904), Yorkshire and England. Shared many a century opening stand with John Tunnicliffe: indeed, at one stage their 554-run partnership against Derbyshire in 1898 was an all-wicket record. Brown scored 300 of those runs. He played from 1889 to 1904, scoring 17,920 runs and appearing in eight Tests. Died at the age of 35 of a heart disease. Postcard by Durhams Ltd., Leeds.

96. W.G. Grace, the man most associated with the game of cricket. A legend in his day while playing for Gloucestershire, London County and England; a legend now for those not even interested in cricket. There does not appear to have been a card published that features him with Gloucester, for whom he played from 1865 to 1899. After a dispute he left to manage the London County team based at the Crystal Palace ground, though happily he did return later. This card shows him leading England against Australia in 1899 at Trent Bridge - his last Test appearance. For Wilfred Rhodes, seated on the ground, left, it was the first of 58 England caps. The postcard was published by the Rotary Photo Co., and postally used in September 1904.

ENGLAND XI
BARLOW (UMPIRE) HAYWARD C. B. FRY HIRST RANJI RHODES GUNN J. T. HEARNE Dr W. G. GRACE STORER BROCKWELL JACKSON TYLDESLEY TITCHMARSH (UMPIRE)

DR. W. G. GRACE. (CAPTAIN) LONDON COUNTY.

97. Captain of London County as shown in the 'Star' series of 1904.

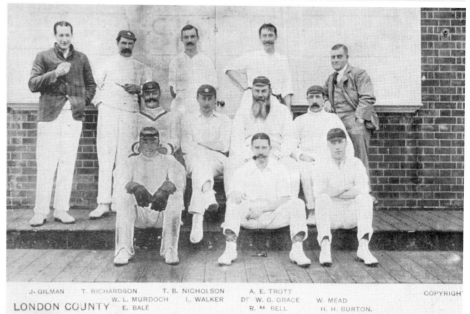

LONDON COUNTY
J. GILMAN T. RICHARDSON T. B. NICHOLSON A. E. TROTT W. L. MURDOCH L. WALKER Dr W. G. GRACE W. MEAD E. BALE R. M. BELL H. H. BURTON.

98. The London County XI, 1904, led by W.G. Grace, and including many famous players. Mead of Essex, and the Australians Murdoch and Trott are among those featured on this 'Star' series postcard.

SOUTH OF ENGLAND XI v THE AUSTRALIAN
TITCHMARSH (UMPIRE) BROCKWELL C. B. FRY TOWNSEND LOCKWOOD G. JESSOP GRACE MASON RANJI BOARD HAYWARD ABEL WEST

99. The South of England XI, led by W.G., at the Crystal Palace in 1899, where they played the Australian tourists in their opening game - a draw. Gregory and Noble both scored centuries for the visitors. The card was published by Rotary, and the message on the back reads: *"I should send card on to Mr. Abel if I was you. Yours truly, W.H. Lockwood. P.S. Kensington Oval will find him."*

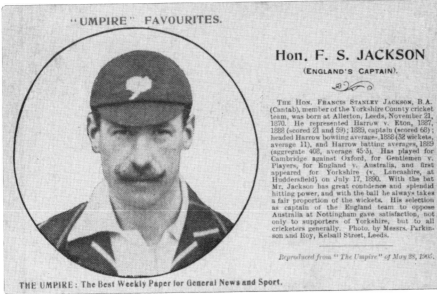

The postcard was not only a form of communication, and a device for recording events, but was also used as an advertising medium, as the cards featured here show.

100. (above). F.S. Jackson, the England captain of 1905, as featured in the "Umpire", a popular sporting paper of the day.

101. This self-explanatory card was produced by Arthur Shrewsbury and Arthur Shaw the famous bowler who had a sports shop on Carrington Street, Nottingham.

102. Summers, Brown and Company patented the 'Force' cricket bat, and produced a series of postcards based on photographs by C. Debenham, London, with testimonies from players of the day, including Humphreys (illustrated), Tarrant, Seymour and Strudwick.

103. The Australian captain, Warwick Armstrong, as portrayed by the Jaeger Company. This particular postcard was used as a handout by their agent, Vivian Brothers.

104. Jack Hobbs went to Australia to report on the M.C.C. tour of 1932-3 for the *Star* newspaper. This card was presumably produced by the paper itself.

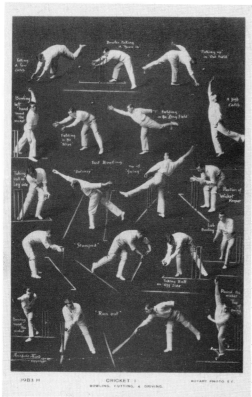

105. An instructional card published by the Rotary Photo Co., series 3983 H.

106. Five cricketers of the year, 1923. Published by Frank Smith, High St., Oxford.

107. This card, published by W.H. Smith in their 'Grosvenor' series, shows the popularity of the players of the day in that J.T. Tyldesley's birthplace was reckoned to be of interest!

FACING PAGE:

108. Clem Hill (1877-1945), South Australia and Australia. A Valentine series card of the 1905 tourist, a fine left-hand bat who scored 3,412 runs for Australia in 49 Tests, and in his career (1892-1923) accumulated 17,213 runs with 45 centuries. This card was posted in Melbourne in January 1907.

109. Sidney E. Gregory (1870-1929), New South Wales and Australia. A superb batsman and excellent fielder who played 58 times for Australia and was captain in 1912. From 1899 to 1913, he scored 15,192 runs, including 25 centuries. Millar and Lang 'National' series no. 829.

110. Joe Darling (1870-1946), South Australia and Australia. He toured England four times (1896, 1899, 1902 and 1905) and was captain on all but the first visit. Darling could be classed as one of Australia's great left-hand bats. In all cricket from 1893 to 1907, he scored 10,635 runs, appearing in 34 Test matches. Card published by Valentine of Dundee.

111. Warwick W. Armstrong (1879-1947), Victoria and Australia. The 'big ship', as he was known, is the only Australian to have scored 2,000 runs and taken 100 wickets on an English tour. From 1898 to 1921, he made 16,158 runs and took 832 wickets - one of Australia's greatest captains. Another Valentine postcard.

112. Monty A. Noble (1873-1940), New South Wales and Australia. A fine all-rounder, perhaps the best ever produced by Australia. He played 42 Test matches, and was captain in 1903-4 and 1907-8. From 1893 to 1919 he scored 13,975 runs, including 37 centuries and took 625 wickets. Card published by Raphael Tuck, one of a set of six titled *In the Open - Famous Fielders'*, no. 6452.

113. Warren Bardsley (1882-1954), New South Wales and Australia. An accomplished left-hand opening bat who in 41 Tests scored 2,469 runs including six centuries. He first played for N.S.W. in 1903, and up to 1926 made 17,025 runs. This postcard was published by Millar and Lang in their 'National' series, no. 829.

114. Victor V. Trumper (1877-1915), New South Wales and Australia. The 'immortal' Australian cricketer on a Millar and Lang postcard (same series as previous card). He scored 16,939 runs in a career from 1894-1913, and made 48 appearances for his country.

108

109

110

111

Mr. M. A. NOBLE.   "A CATCH AT POINT."

112

113

114

COMIC CARDS

Comic picture postcards based on a cricketing theme were extremely popular in Edwardian England, and the selection featured on pages 36-38 include examples of the work of some of the most famous cartoonists of the period.

115. No publisher is identified on this interpretation by artist E.J.W. of the popular Edwardian catch-phrase 'Tom Bowling'. The postcard was sent from Reading in August 1904.

116. Lance Thackeray produced many fine designs for picture postcards, illustrating most facets of life. Two cricket series were included in his repertoire, in the Raphael Tuck "write-away" style. This is from series 983, Thackeray's pictorial representation of "I hope to catch you ..." Posted in Forest Gate, London in October 1903.

117. Cricket cartoon with a political flavour; 1905 vintage, publisher unknown. Joseph Chamberlain is at the wicket, batting away for tariff reform.

118. W.G. Grace by Thackeray. "I should like to play you at ping-pong ..." Tuck 'write-away' series 624. Posted at Liscard, Cheshire, in August 1902.

119. A very early 'write-away' type using cricketing situation. No publisher - probably a privately-produced card in limited quantity.

120. An interesting interpretation of a cricketing phrase. A Valentine's publication.

121. Another 'write-away'. Was this the inspiration for Kerry Packer's duck caricature on his Australian Channel 9 television coverage? Valentine's series 545.

122. "Our Demon Bowler" on a comic card drawn by Donald McGill, and published by Joseph Asher and Co. Ltd. in their 'Kismet' series (no. 281). McGill is more famous for the seaside comics he drew from 1904 until the 1950's. The postcard is of 1907 vintage, but it wasn't actually postally used till October 1916 - and then from a Field Post Office on the Western Front.

WELL HELD, OR A LONG SLIP.

123. Rene Bull was one of the members of the London Sketch Club, a fraternity of cartoonists that provided much material for magazines and postcards. Posted at Swanage in August 1905, this comes from Davidson Bros' series 6136.

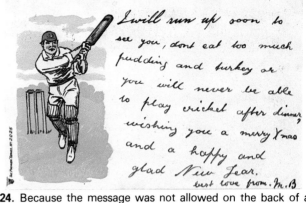

I will run up soon to see you, don't eat too much pudding and turkey or you will never be able to play cricket after dinner, wishing you a merry Xmas and a happy and glad New Year. best love from. M. B

124. Because the message was not allowed on the back of a postcard before 1902, space was at a premium for picture and words on the front. Many comic cards thus used a vignette picture and 'write-away' techniques, where the first few words of a message were provided for the sender. On this card, in the 'Premier' series (no. 2025) these were *"I will run up ..."* The writer has added his own message.

GOING IN.   TOM. B.

125. Tom Browne's depiction of the walk to the wicket - this monocled gentleman looks anything but nervous, though. Card sent from Waterloo, Liverpool, in November 1905.

"COMIC CRICKET."

Always keep your "eye on the ball."

126. "Keep your eye on the ball" was a phrase frequently used by comic artists. This postcard was published by Misch and Stock in their 'Comic Cricket' series no. 180.

Jimmie (to college boy who has come out with a couple of ducks): "D'ye mind givin' us yer 'autograft,' mate?"

127. Unsigned portrayal of an embarrassing situation on a J. Salmon postcard, no. 2982.

AT THE WICKET

O! O!

Merry Christmas Greetings.

128. Another Thackeray cartoon, from Tuck's 'At the Wicket' series 955. A somewhat comprehensive dismissal.

CARRIED HIS BAT.

Cricket Illustrated.

129. 'Cricket Illustrated' by Hebblethwaite. Tuck Oilette postcard 6446, sent from Newcastle-on-Tyne in June 1905.

"I NEARLY MADE A GREAT HIT HERE - BUT ...."

130. A comic card by James Bamforth and Co. Ltd. of Holmfirth, one of the most famous names in English postcard publishing, representing a continuous tradition throughout this century. This example is in the 'Bat' series, no. 806.

131. A familiar scene, drawn by Donald McGill. Published by Joseph Asher and Co., cricket series no. 282, and posted at Wakefield in May 1914. The postcard is addressed to Frank Wardle of the Priory School, Malvern, and the message reads: "Nothing 'personal' is intended, but I thought this rather nice in the cricket line. There has been a match here two Saturdays but too cold to go and watch!"

132. Tom Browne with another "Demon Bowler". This Nottingham-born artist produced hundreds of designs for postcards, most of them published by Davidson Bros. This is from series 2564, one of several illustrating cricket phrases or situations. Browne was adept at capturing behaviour in a succinct sketch.

133. Millar and Lang, art publishers of Glasgow and London, produced a series of six cricket cartoons by an unidentified artist in 1907. This is one of them, posted at Bristol in September of that year.

134. A collision in mid-wicket. Postcard published by Ernest Nister, London (series 77), and posted at Andover in July 1905. Message reads: *"How do you like this? This is what happens sometimes in our cricket ..."*

135. Illustrating cricket phrases was a favourite trick of Edwardian cartoonists. No evidence as to who drew this one, but the card - one of a set of six - was published by Valentine's of Dundee.

136. Another card by Valentine's of Dundee, postally used in 1911. A cricketing situation is used to illustrate a contemporary catch-phrase.

137. Joseph Asher and Co.'s "Cricket Series" no. 290, a set of six postcards by Donald McGill, illustrating various laws.

138. Another Tom Browne cartoon, published by Geo. Newnes Ltd. for 'Captain' magazine.

139. Strudwick (Surrey), Hayward (Surrey), Braund (Somerset), Lilley (Warwickshire).

140. Arnold (Worcestershire), Relf (Sussex), Fielder (Kent), Knight (Leicestershire).

141. Bosanquet (Middlesex), Warner (Middlesex), Foster (Worcestershire).

The 1903-4 team was the first touring side to visit Australia under the title of M.C.C. It was led by P.F. Warner, and, largely due to his captaincy gained success against players of the calibre of Trumper, Noble and Hill.

The four postcards featuring the tourists shown here were produced anonymously, probably in a sheet, as evidenced by side perforations. A later series of the 1905 Australians was produced for *'The Captain'* boys' magazine, but they were clearly marked as such.

142. Rhodes (Yorkshire), Tyldesley (Lancashire), Hirst (Yorkshire).

THE ENGLAND XI. IN AUSTRALIA, 1904

BRAUND,	RELF,	ARNOLD,	RHODES,	HAYWARD,	
	FIELDER,	HIRST,	STRUDWICK,	KNIGHT,	LILLEY,
	R. E. FOSTER,		P. F. WARNER,	B. J. T. BOSANQUET,	
	TYLDESLEY,				

143. On board the *'Orantes'* bound for Australia, illustrated on a Rotary Photo series postcard. This example is autographed on the front by A.E. Relf (Sussex) and on the reverse by T. Hayward (Surrey).

144. The tourists in Australia, on a photographic postcard published by Broom (series no. 13858).

MR P. F. WARNER'S TEAM.

| G. HIRST, | A.A. LILLEY, | H. STRUDWICK, | A.E. KNIGHT, | W. FIELDER, | A.E. RELF, | W. RHODES, | T. HAYWARD, |
| | E. ARNOLD, | R.E. FOSTER, | | P.F. WARNER, | J.T. TYLDESLEY, | L.C. BRAUND. | |

BROOM 13858

Below: Three of the 1903-4 M.C.C. team in Australia.

A. FIELDER (KENT)

145. A. Fielder (Kent), on a card published by J. Mockford.

ARNOLD. (WORCESTERSHIRE) LONDON E.C. 1234

146. E. Arnold (Worcestershire). A postcard by Rapid Photo Co., posted at Manchester in May 1904.

147. T. Hayward (Surrey) - again, no publisher indicated.

PHILCO SERIES 6207 D

FIELDER	HAYES		HARDSTAFF	BARNES
J. N. CRAWFORD	K. L. HUTCHINGS	A. O. JONES	F. L. FANE	R. A. YOUNG
BRAUND	HUMPHRIES	HOBBS	BLYTHE	RHODES

148. The M.C.C. team which toured Australia in 1907-8 won seven and drew eight of its nineteen games. A.O. Jones of Nottinghamshire was the appointed captain, but after the fifth match - against Queensland - he became seriously ill, and Frederick Fane captained the side for eight matches, including three Tests. Card published by the Philco Publishing Co., London, series no. 6207 D.

149. An attractively-designed postcard by the Pictorial Postcard Co., London, featuring the 1907-8 tourists.

150. A similar effort from the Rotary Photo Co., series no. 3827A.

OFFICERS MESS CIGARETTES

ENGLISH TEAM 1913-1914.

151. This touring M.C.C. side won twelve, drew nine, and lost only one of its games. Though not strictly a postcard - rather a postcard-size cigarette card - this publication of Officers Mess Cigarettes shows the team captained by J.W.H.T. Douglas. It includes Frank Woolley and Jack Hobbs (on the back row) and Wilfred Rhodes (seated, right).

Below: Two of the most experienced players who went on this tour.

152. A.E. Relf (1874-1937), Sussex and England. Played in 22 matches on the tour, capturing 48 wickets at an average of 20.29, and scoring 503 runs including 106 against a Northern Natal side. Card published by F. Hartmann.

H. STRUDWICK, SURREY.
WICKETKEEPER.

153. H. Strudwick (1880-1970), Surrey and England. Played in all five Test matches, catching 15 and stumping 6 batsmen. John Walker & Co. of London published the postcard.

"THE TEAM WHO BROUGHT BACK THE ASHES." *1928-29.*

Front Row— E. Tyldesley, J. C. White, A. P. F. Chapman, D. R. Jardine, Jack Hobbs.
Middle Row— M. Leyland, S. J. Staples, W. Hammond, F. C. Toone (manager), H. Sutcliffe, Larwood, A. P. Freeman.
Back Row— T. Duckworth, L. Ames, C. P. Mead, M. W. Tate, E. Hendren.

154. The successful England tourists to Australia in 1928-9, captained by A.P.F. Chapman (Kent). It was during this tour that a young Australian called Don Bradman first made his mark. Publisher of the card unknown. The side won ten games, drew thirteen, and lost one.

155. The M.C.C. team to Australia, 1932-33, captained by Douglas Jardine. The tour attracted a considerable amount of controversy, mainly through the 'leg theory' bowling of the Englishmen in an effort to curtail Bradman's run-scoring. Publisher of the card - complete with facsimile signatures - unknown. The tourists won ten, drew thirteen, tied one, and lost one of twenty-five games.

Below: Three members of the 1932-33 M.C.C. side.

156. Maurice Leyland (Yorkshire). Photo postcard by T.A. Cornall, Harrogate.

157. Harold Larwood (Nottinghamshire). Photo postcard by Jack Webb, Nottingham.

158. Herbert Sutcliffe (Yorkshire). Card published by the *Yorkshire Observer*.

DR. W. G. GRACE.

159. W.G. Grace (1848-1915), Gloucestershire, London County and England. In 22 matches for his country, he scored 1,098 runs including two centuries, but surprisingly taking only nine wickets. He captained England on many occasions during the 1880's and 1890's, scoring the first century in Test matches in England - 152 against Australia in 1880. Postcard published by Wrench, series no. 2931.

161. A.C. Maclaren (1871-1944), Lancashire and England. Succeeding W.G. Grace as captain of England in 1899 (against Australia), he went on to lead his country again in 1902 and 1909, and also took his own team to Australia in 1901-2. In 35 Tests, Maclaren scored 1,931 runs, averaging 33.87, including five hundreds. Card published by Rotary Photo Co., series no. 3812.

P. F. WARNER, MIDDLESEX. BATSMAN (CAPTAIN).

The English Cricketers who won the "Ashes" from the Australians March 3rd 1904

160. P.F. Warner (1873-1963), Oxford, Middlesex and England. Despite his delicate nature, Pelham Warner was a cricket pioneer in every sense. He led the first M.C.C. team to Australia in 1903-4, returning with the 'Ashes', and the first M.C.C. side to South Africa in 1905-6 - a Test disaster. In all, he played in 15 Tests, scoring 622 runs. A John Walker postcard.

Hon. F. S. JACKSON, Captain of the English Team.

162. F.S. Jackson (1870-1947), Cambridge, Yorkshire and England, on an anonymously-published card. He was captain of England during the 1905 season when he successfully led England to victory (two wins, three draws), in the series against the Australians, retaining the 'Ashes'. In 20 Tests, he scored 1,415 runs, including five centuries. Card published anonymously.

Mr. A. O. Jones

The Wrench Series. No. 1694

163. A.O. Jones (1872-1914), Cambridge, Not-tinghamshire and England. Captain of the 1907-8 tourists to Australia, though dogged by ill-health during the visit. Never did justice to Test cricket, but a brilliant county player; he died of tuber-culosis in 1914. A Wrench series (no. 1694) postcard.

C.B. FRY

Produced in Berlin

164. C.B. Fry (1872-1956), Oxford, Sussex, Lon-don County, Hampshire and England. Captained his country to success in the triangular tournament of 1912 against Australia and South Africa. A brilliant man - both on and off the sporting field - he scored 1,223 runs (with two centuries) in 26 Tests. A Giesen Brothers postcard.

R.E.FOSTER

165. R.E. Foster (1878-1914), Worcestershire and England. The only one of the famous Foster brothers to represent his country, 'R.E.' captained England against South Africa in 1907, winning one test and drawing the other two. He played in eight Tests, averaging 46.30. Sadly, Foster died of diabetes at the age of 36. A photographic postcard published by Foster of Brighton.

MR. J. W. H. T. DOUGLAS

CAPTN. OF ENGLAND, 1911-12   CAPTN. OF ESSEX, 1911-12

166. J.W.H.T. Douglas (1882-1930), Essex and England. Tragically drowned while trying to save his father in a sea accident in 1930, Johnny Douglas played 23 Tests for England, being cap-tain in 18 of them. He played for Essex from 1901 to 1928, scoring a total of 24,531 runs and taking 1,893 wickets. This postcard is from a particularly attractive series published locally in Leyton by C. Agar.

167. The Australian tourists of 1902, on a card published by Giesen brothers. They played 39 games, winning 23, losing two, and drawing fourteen. Despite an atrocious start to the tour, due to rain day after day, the tourists proved to be one of the most successful overseas teams ever to visit England, comparing with the 1921 and 1948 Australians. On the 1902 tour, Victor Trumper was magnificent, despite the weather, and scored 2,570 runs, including eleven centuries.

168. R.A. Duff (1878-1911), New South Wales and Australia. A very punishing right-hand bat who first played for N.S.W. in 1898, he scored a total of 6,589 runs and appeared in 22 Tests for Australia. Card published by R. Dunn, series no. 1014.

169. J.J. Kelly (1867-1938), New South Wales and Australia. An outstanding wicket-keeper who appeared in 36 Tests, touring England four times, last in 1905. He played for his state from 1894 to 1906, dismissing 355 batsmen in all. Postcard by T. Bolland, Southall.

The 1905 Australian tourists to England were probably the most widely-covered team on picture postcards. That year was about the height of the Edwardian postcard boom. Here we see four examples of the variety of cards that could be bought during that tour.

170. Philco photographic series no. 6003F.

171. Rapid Photo Co. series no. 2337.

172. Photocrom Co. Ltd., London.

173. W.H. Smith 'Grosvenor' series.

Three further permutations of the 1905 Australian tourists. Possibly by the end of the summer of 1905, the cricketing public would know these faces as well as their best friends!

174. Hartmann & Co. postcard.

175. This card was published in Nottingham by H. Lindley, no doubt for sale at Trent Bridge during the Test that began on the 29th May, 1905. A similar souvenir card was published to co-incide with the Lords Test of June 15th-17th.

176. A postcard published in Melbourne, Australia, by Alice Wills. It was sent *'via Frisco'* to Mr. S. Cleasley, Stockport, and asked him *"to look out for yourselves at Old Trafford - Tyldesley will have to be at his best."*

H. CARTER (The Australian Cricket Team 1909.)

177. H. Carter (New South Wales and Australia).

C. G. MACARTNEY (The Australian Cricket Team 1909.)

178. C.G. Macartney (New South Wales and Australia).

P. A. McALISTER (The Australian Cricket Team 1909.)

179. P.A. McAlister (Victoria and Australia).

180. The 1909 Australian tourists, photographed and published by T. Bolland. Led by Monty Noble, the tourists played 39 games, winning 13, losing 4, and drawing 22.

Davidson Brothers produced a real photographic series of cards, each depicting one of the 1909 tourists. Nine of them are featured on this and the next page.

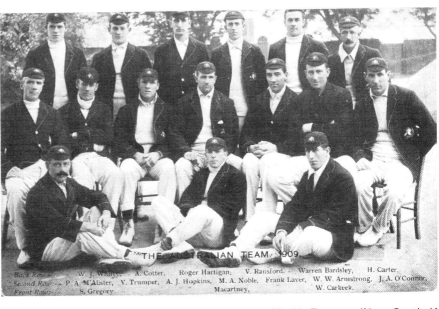

THE AUSTRALIAN TEAM. 1909.

Back Row: W. J. Whitty, A. Cotter, Roger Hartigan, V. Ransford, Warren Bardsley, H. Carter. Second Row: P. A. M'Alister, V. Trumper, A. J. Hopkins, M. A. Noble, Frank Laver, W. W. Armstrong, J. A. O'Connor. Front Row: S. Gregory, Macartney, W. Carkeek.

181. W.W. Armstrong (Victoria and Australia).

182. V.S. Ransford (Victoria and Australia).

183. V. Trumper (New South Wales and Australia).

W. W. ARMSTRONG (The Australian Cricket Team 1909.)

V. S. RANSFORD (The Australian Cricket Team 1909.)

V. T. TRUMPER (The Australian Cricket Team 1909.)

W. BARDSLEY (The Australian Cricket Team 1909.)

184. W. Bardsley (New South Wales and Australia).

W. J. WHITTY (The Australian Cricket Team 1909.)

185. W.J. Whitty (New South Wales, South Australia and Australia).

A. J. HOPKINS (The Australian Cricket Team 1909.)

186. A.J. Hopkins (New South Wales and Australia).

333.T.   BEAGLES' POSTCARDS

THE AUSTRALIAN CRICKET TEAM, 1912.

C.J. CROUCH (Manager), R.B. MINNETT, E. HUME (Visitor), C. KELLEWAY, E.R. MAYNE, S.H. EMERY, D. SMITH, W.J. WHITTY, H. WEBSTER, G.R. HAZLITT.
W. BARDSLEY, J.W. McLAREN, T.J. MATTHEWS, S.E. GREGORY (Capt.), C.B. JENNINGS (Vice-Capt.), C.G. MACARTNEY, W. CARKEEK.

187. The 1912 Australian touring side, led by S.E. Gregory. Of the 38 scheduled matches, they won nine, lost eight and drew twenty. One was abandoned. This is a Beagles-published postcard, series no. 333T

188. Another card of the 1912 Australians, this time by T. Bolland. Whilst not a particularly good tour for the visitors, two of their batsmen, Warren Bardsley (seated, third right), and Charles Macartney (seated, second right) both had excellent seasons: Bardsley scored 2,441 runs (eight hundreds), and Macartney 2,207 (six centuries). Both Whitty and Hazlitt took over a hundred wickets.

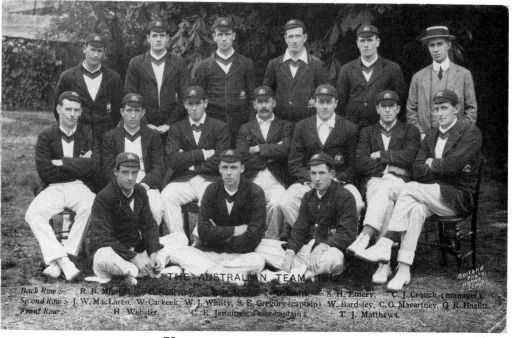

THE AUSTRALIAN TEAM

Back Row :   R. B. Minnett,   C. Kelleway,   D. Smith,   E. R. Mayne,   S. H. Emery,   C. J. Crouch, (manager).
Second Row :   J. W. MacLaren,   W. Carkeek,   W. J. Whitty,   S. E. Gregory (captain),   W. Bardsley,   C.G. Macartney,   G. R. Hazlitt.
Front Row :   H. Webster,   C. B. Jennings (vice-captain),   T. J. Matthews.

The Australian tourists in England between the two World Wars.

Looking at the overall record in England - Australia Tests between 1920 and 1938 (England won 15, Australia won 22, and 12 were drawn) it would seem that the Aussies held the upper hand. Thirteen of their victories, though, came in the early part of the 1920's, when English international cricket was at a low ebb, and Australia had such strong bowling talent as McDonald, Gregory and Mailey. In 1926, England turned the corner, winning one and drawing four of the Tests, and going on to retain the 'Ashes' in 1928-9. The 1930 tourists brought the talents of Bradman and Jackson, and Australia won the series two-one, before England, under Douglas Jardine, and spearheaded by Larwood and Voce, sensationally triumphed in Australia by four Tests to one. This was the last time the 'Ashes' were won by England prior to 1939, for the Aussies won the rubbers in England (1934), Australia (1936-7), and England again (1938).

Of the five teams shown here, the 1921 tourists had by far the best playing record. How far the Great War had affected English cricket is debatable, though bad selections, loss of form, and injuries also played their part. Nevertheless, Warwick Armstrong was an excellent captain of a splendid team. They are compared favourably with the touring sides of 1902 and 1948.

189. The 1921 Australians were led by Warwick Armstrong, and featured on this Rotary Photo Co. postcard.

190. H.L. Collins captained the 1926 touring side. This card was published by T. Bolland, St. Leonards-on-Sea.

191. J. Smith, the Bookstall, Lords, produced this photographic card of the 1930 Australian tourists, captained by W.W. Woodfull.

192. Woodfull was captain again for the 1934 trip. Postcard by Photo-works Ltd., Brighouse.

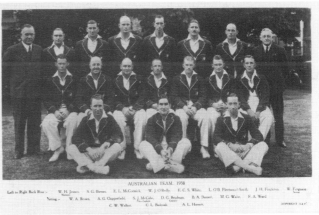

193. The 1938 Australian tourists, captained by Don Bradman.

ALL-INDIA CRICKET TEAM, 1932

Top row left to right—Lall Singh, P. E. Palia, Jahangir Khan, Mahomed Nisar, Amar Singh, B. E. Kapadia, S. R. Godambe, Ghulam Mahomed, J. G. Navle
Centre—Syed Wazir Ali, Capt. C. K. Nayudu, H.H. Maharaja Porbandar (*Capt.*), K. S. C. Limdi (*Vice-Capt.*), Syed Nazir Ali, Capt. Joginder Singh
Bottom—Naoomal Jeoomal, S. H. M. Colah, N. D. Marshall

194. The first All-India cricket team, other than the Parsees, to visit England was in 1911, and it can safely be said that the second party - pictured above on a Hills and Lacy postcard - was considerably more successful. This latter side played 26 first-class games, winning nine, drawing nine, and losing eight. In their only Test match, at Lords, they lost by 158 runs, but generally made a good impression. Their leading players were C.K. Nayudu, the best batsman in the team, who hit five centuries, and Amar Singh, who captured 111 wickets at an average of 20.78.

ALL INDIA CRICKET TEAM, ENGLAND 1936
(*Left to Right*)
Standing, Back: **M. Baqa Jilani, M. J. Gopalan, L. P. Jai, L. Amar Nath, Amir Elahi, G. Ramaswami**
Sitting: **V. M. Merchant, M. Nisar, C. K. Nayudu, M. K. of Vizianagram, Syed Wazir Ali, P. E. Palia, S. M. Hussain**
(*Captain*)
Front on Ground: **Mushtaq Ali, D. D. Hindlekar, S. Banerjee, K. R. Meher-Homji**

195. It may well have been the cold and wet weather of the 1936 season that prevented the 1936 All-India team from doing themselves justice. Playing 28 first-class matches, they won only four, drawing twelve, and losing the remaining twelve fixtures. Two of three Tests were lost, and one drawn. V.M. Merchant was easily the leading batsman, scoring 1,745 runs in three-day games at an average of 51.32. A real photographic postcard by Norvic Mill.

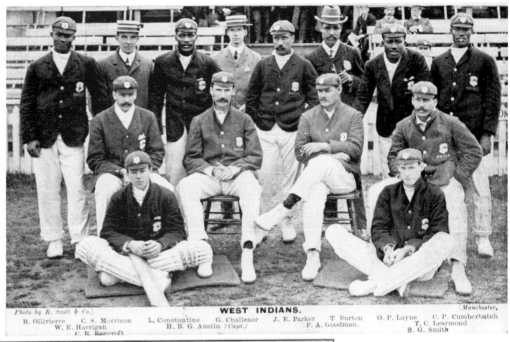

196. West Indian tourists of 1906 on a postcard published by R. Scott, Manchester. Under H.G.B. Austin, they played thirteen first-class matches, winning three, drawing two, and losing eight. At times, they were a match for some of the counties, their win over a weakened Yorkshire by 262 runs raising a few eyebrows. On the back row is the great George Challenor, a highly-regarded batsman, and, next to him, Constantine, the father of the more famous Sir Leary.

Photo by R. Scott & Co.] **WEST INDIANS.** [Manchester.
R. Ollivierre   C. S. Morrison   L. Constantine   G. Challenor   J. E. Parker   T. Burton   O. P. Layne   C. P. Cumberbatch
W. E. Harrigan   H. B. G. Austin (Capt.)   P. A. Goodman   T. C. Learmond
C. R. Bancroft   S. G. Smith

Back Row- **"WEST INDIES CRICKET TEAM."**
left to right - W. St. Hill, E. A. Rae, E. L. G. Hoad, J. A. Small, F. R. Martin, L. S. Constantine, J. Neblett,
Sitting left to right- L. E. Bartlett, M. P. Fernandes, C. V. Wight, R. K. Nunes, G. Challinor, C. R. Brown.
Published by- Bookstalls, Lords & Oval.   Printed by- B. P. Co. Ltd. London.

197. R.K. Nunes led the West Indian touring side of 1928, the first side from the Caribbean to play Tests against England. They actually lost all three by an innings, though. Five out of 30 first-class games produced victories for the tourists, and of their remaining games, they drew thirteen and lost twelve. By far the leading light of the team - 1,381 runs and 107 wickets - was Leary Constantine. This postcard was published by the Lords and Oval bookstalls.

198. The 1933 team, led by G.C. Grant, enjoyed a very hot summer, though this was not reflected in their performances - five matches were won, sixteen drawn, and nine lost. Easily the star of the team was George Headley, a batsman who came with a high reputation, disappointed no-one, and scored 2,320 runs with seven centuries.

WEST INDIES CRICKET TEAM, 1933
LEFT TO RIGHT. STANDING- E. MARTINDALE, F. R. MARTIN, C. MERRY, V. A. VALENTINE, I. BARROW, O DA COSTA, E. ACHONG
SITTING- H. C. GRIFFITH, E. L. G. HOAD, J. M. KIDNEY (MNGR), G. C. GRANT (CAPT), C. A. WILES, C. A. ROACH
FRONT- B. SEALY, C. M. CHRISTIANI, G. HEADLEY

Copyright photograph by ALEX WATKINSON, A.R.P.S.

199. Sir Leary Constantine (1902-1971), Trinidad, Barbados and West Indies. A dynamic batsman, brilliant fielder, and - at his best - an extremely fast bowler. In a career from 1922 to 1945, he scored 4,451 runs and took 424 wickets; he appeared in eighteen Tests. Card published by A. Watkinson.

WEST INDIES CRICKET TEAM, ENGLAND, 1939

Standing :- W. Ferguson, G. Gomez, J. B. Stollmeyer, L. G. Hylton, T. Johnson, C. B. Clarke, H. P. Bayley, E. A. V. Williams
Sitting :- G. Headley, I. Barrow, R. S. Grant, J. M. Kidney, J. H. Cameron, L. N. Constantine, E. A. Martindale
Front :- K. H. Weekes, J. E. D. Sealey, V. H. Stollmeyer

200. The last West Indies touring team prior to the Second World War came in 1939, led by Rolph Grant, a most capable all-round sportsman. They played 25 first-class matches, winning eight, losing six, and drawing eleven. Publisher of the card unspecified.

J. A. FAULKNER (South Africans)

201. The 1907 South African tourists to England - seen here on a card by R. Scott of Manchester - surprised everyone by their fine all-round cricket, especially strong in the bowling of Schwarz, Vogler, Faulkner and White, all improvising on the 'googly' patented by B.J. Bosanquet. They played three Tests, drawing two and losing one.

202. G.A. Faulkner (1881-1930), Transvaal and South Africa. A most capable all-round cricketer who appeared in 25 Tests for his country. Off the field, he distinguished himself as a soldier, winning the D.S.O. in World War One. Postcard published by Gale and Polden, Southampton.

203. S.J. Pegler (1888-1972), Transvaal and South Africa. A fine spin bowler who played in sixteen Tests, taking 47 wickets at an average of 33.44. He was manager of the 1951 South African touring team to England. The card is from Hawkins of Brighton.

THE SOUTH AFRICAN CRICKET TEAM PHOTOGRAPHED AT LORD'S. [Photo by Central News]
Back Row (left to right): C. Stricker, R. O. Schwarz, R. Beaumont, T. Campbell, G. P. D. Hartigan, J. D. Cox.
Middle Row (left to right): S. J. Pegler, L. J. Tancred, F. Mitchell (Captain), G. Faulkner, S. J. Snooke, A. D. Nourse.
Front Row (left to right): H. W. Taylor, Ward, G. P. Carter.

204. The South African cricket team in England, 1912 - they arrived to take part in a triangular tournament with the host country and Australia. They were led by Frank Mitchell, who previously played for Yorkshire and England, but did not have a very successful time, losing five of the six Tests played and drawing the other. Card published by L. Sales and Sons, Kennington Oval.

PUBLISHED BY
C. SMITH., OVAL, 1924.
THE SOUTH AFRICANS
P. A. M. HANDS. R. H. CATTERALL. C. D. DIXON. M. J. SUSSKIND. E. P. NUPEN. H. G. DEANE. G. F. BISSETT. A. D. NOURSE.
N. PEGLER. M. J. COMMAILLE. H. W. TAYLOR. J. M. BLANCKENBERG. G. HEARNE.
T. A. WARD. D. J. MEINTJES. C. P. CARTER.

205. The South Africans, 1924. At the time this tour was as disappointing as the summer's weather. They won only eight games, losing nine and drawing twenty-one, twelve of these unfinished due to rain. This postcard shows the tourists at the Oval and was produced by J. Beagles and Co. of London. Their captain for this game was H.W. Taylor; Dave Nourse, father of the later more famous Dudley, is at the right on the back row.

206. Five years later, the 1929 tourists proved marginally more successful, but were still unable to win a Test in England. Two were lost, and three drawn. The card, published by J. Smith, includes H.B. Cameron, a wicketkeeper batsman of extreme high class. This side was led by H.G. Deane.

THE SOUTH AFRICAN CRICKET TEAM, 1929.
L. to R. standing back row - SIEDLE. B. MITCHELL. A. L. OCHSE. A. J. BELL. | Middle row sitting - H. B. CAMERON. H. W. TAYLOR. C. FRELINGHAUS
D. P. B. MORKEL. A. J. CHRISTY. N. A. QUINN. Q. McMILLAN, | (Manager). H. G. DEANE. (Captain). R. H. CATTERALL. C. L. VINCENT.
E. L. DALTON. H. FRAMES. (Secretary). | In front - E. G. OWEN-SMITH and E. W. VAN DER MERWE.

SOUTH AFRICAN CRICKET TEAM. ENGLAND 1935
Standing: R. J. Williams, K. G. Viljoen, E. A. B. Rowan, D. S. Tomlinson, R. J. Crisp, A. B. Langton, A. D. Nourse, X. Balaskas.
Sitting: I. J. Siedle, C. L. Vincent, H. B. Cameron, S. J. Snooke, H. F. Wade, B. Mitchell, A. J. Bell, E. L. Dalton.
V. CAPT. MNGR. CAPT.
COPYRIGHT A.W.S.

207. Led by H.F. Wade, the 1935 South Africans at last won a Test in England; in fact they took the series, with the other four drawn. Comparisons were made with the strong 1907 outfit, and they won 17 of 31 first-class games, losing only two. On returning home, Cameron caught enteric fever and died at the age of thirty.

THE NEW ZEALAND CRICKET TEAM.

Back Row: W. Cunningham, C. J. Oliver, W. E. Merritt, M. Henderson, K. C. James, J. E. Mills, C. F. W. Allcott.
Front: M. L. Page, C. C. Dacre, T. C. Lowry (Capt.), R. C. Blunt, C. S. Demster, H. M. McGirr, Absent, E. H. L. Bernau.
Photo: Topical.

208. The first New Zealand touring team to visit England was captained by T.C. Lowry, and arrived in 1927. They played 26 first-class games, winning seven, losing five, and drawing fourteen - a most commendable record for a team of modest ability.

OFFICIAL PHOTOGRAPH   NEW ZEALAND TEST TEAM 1931.

Left to right Standing—I. B. CROMB, J. L. KERR, K. C. JAMES, R. O. TALBOT, G. L. WEIR, W. E. MERRITT, A. M. MATHESON.
Left to right Sitting—J. E. MILLS,   M. L. PAGE,   T. C. LOWRY,   C. F. W. ALLCOTT,   C. S. DEMPSTER.
(Vice Captain)   (Captain)   (Treasurer)
Published by Angus Thomas Ltd.   Left to right Front Row—R. C. BLUNT,   H. G. VIVIAN.

209. The 1931 New Zealand tourists, again led by Lowry, made their Test debuts at Lords and achieved an honourable draw. On the tour, six of 32 first-class games were won, and three lost. Postcard published by Angus Thomas Ltd.

210. In 1937 the New Zealanders had only a moderate tour under M.L. Page, winning nine of their first-class matches, drawing fifteen, and losing nine. Six of the batsmen exceeded a thousand runs, including Martin Donnelly, a future world-class player, and Walter Hadlee. Publisher of the card unknown.

NEW ZEALAND CRICKET TEAM, 1937

T. C. Lowry,   W. N. Carson,   J. Cowie,   N. Gallichan,   W. A. Hadlee,   J. R. Lamason,   J. A. Dunning,   D. A. R. Moloney,   W. Ferguson
Manager   Scorer
E. W. T. Tindill,   A. W. Roberts,   H. G. Vivian,   M. L. Page,   G. L. Weir,   J. L. Kerr.
Vice-Captain   Captain
W. M. Wallace,   M. P. Donnelly

On Saturday, 20th May 1911, the spectators at the Sussex v Nottinghamshire game at Hove took their lunch fully expecting a Sussex victory in the afternoon session - Notts were 260 for 9, only 84 runs ahead in their second innings, with Ted Alletson (47 not out) and W. Riley together. When play resumed, a hitting spectacle moved the score from 260 to 412 in just forty minutes! There was general confusion as to what actually happened, but the final outcome was that Alletson, when caught by C.L.A. Smith, had scored 189 runs in 90 minutes. At one point after lunch he made 115 in seven overs, hitting 'Tim' Killick for 22 in one over and 34 in another (including two no-balls). In all he hit eight sixes, twenty-three fours, four threes, ten two's, and seventeen singles.

Players on both sides were amazed at the power of his shots, and many of the fielders - some hardened internationals - admitted fear of being in the firing line. The magazine *Cricketer* of May 27th 1911, reporting this phenomenon, actually suggested that Killick should be envied for his bowling record and must have enjoyed the fun as much as Alletson and the crowd - I doubt it!

The match finished in a draw, Sussex being 213 for 9 at the close, 24 short of victory.

On the next playing day, Alletson went in at Bristol and hit 60 runs in half-an-hour. One or two more 'Jessop'-type innings secured him a test trial; he also hit Wilfred Rhodes for three successive sixes - no mean feat - and in 1913, in his last full season of county cricket, joined the Lords playing staff. After two games in 1914, he retired at the age of 30.

211. E.B. Alletson (1884-1963), Nottinghamshire. Despite his glorious 189 against Sussex, this was to be his only century in first-class cricket. In his career, from 1906-1914 he scored only 3,217 runs (average 18.59) and took 33 wickets (average 19.03). This postcard was published in the 'Cobden' series by R. Henson & Co., Nottingham.

212. E.H. Killick (1875-1948), Sussex. A fine all-round cricketer, from 1893-1913 he scored 18,768 runs and took 729 wickets. He was the chief 'victim' of Alletson's assault. Card published by Wrench, series no. 1382.

An Oval Record.

Record scores and partnerships would attract immediate attention, and the feat would be on a postcard within days, to be placed in the cricketing fanatic's album for posterity.

213. Jack Hobbs and Andy Sandham, who shared in 66 century partnerships for Surrey, put on 428 for the first wicket against Oxford University at the Oval in June 1926. Sandham, who was first out, scored 183, and Hobbs 261; these scores were made over three days in a drawn match badly affected by rain. The card was published by C.E. Smith, the bookstall, The Oval.

214. The stand of 555 for the first wicket by Herbert Sutcliffe and Percy Holmes, against Essex at Leyton in 1932, beat by one run the previous record by their Yorkshire predecessors, J.T. Brown and John Tunnicliffe. This new record stood for 45 years before being broken in a game in Pakistan. The card was published anonymously.

215. On Tuesday, 6th July 1909, at Stourbridge, Kent were 320 for 9 in response to Worcestershire's total of 360 when Albert Fielder, Kent's last man, joined not out batsman Frank Woolley, with an hour's play left. At the close they'd added 119, and the next morning a further hour and twenty minutes saw the total rise to 555 before Woolley gave a catch to H.K. Foster off Arnold's bowling. He had made 185, Fielder was 112 not out, and they'd added 235 runs for the last wicket - still a record in the County Championship. At the time this was a career-best for Woolley, and Fielder's only century. With a lead of 125, Kent went on to bowl Worcester out for 162, winning by an innings and 33 runs; Colin Blythe took 7-44. The card was published by J. Mockford of Tonbridge.

216. At Hove, between August 5th and 8th, 1933, Sussex crushed Middlesex by an innings and 65 runs, losing only three wickets in the process. The victory was almost entirely due to a record first-wicket partnership for Sussex between Ted Bowley (283) and John Langridge (195) of 490. Middlesex, despite a fine innings of 79 by Patsy Hendren in their first knock, and 80 by Gubby Allen out of 157 in the second innings, were well-beaten early on the morning of the third day. Postcard by an unidentified publisher.

217. Sir E.D. Walker and R. Wood's team against W. Bucknell's XI, taken at an unknown date and location. There are several Yorkshire county players on view including Rhodes, Haigh and Hirst. Card published by S. & A.P. Co., D. Another mystery!

SIR ED WALKER AND R. WOOD'S TEAM VERSUS U. BUCKNELL'S XI.

218. The 1921 Australian team against Cumberland on a postcard postally used on September 17th of that year and sent by H.S., one of the crowd in the picture. Published by Romney Studios of Whitehaven.

219. Sir Julien Cahn was a great benefactor of Nottinghamshire cricket in the 1920's and 1930's. For many years he had his own team, attracting - as is obvious from the names on this card - many famous international players. For many years after retiring from a long first-class career for Nottinghamshire, John Gunn assisted him, and D.P.B. Morkel, an all-rounder who played 16 times for South Africa, set up a successful motor business in Nottingham under Sir Julien's guidance. The postcard, published by the Times of Ceylon Co. Ltd., shows the 1937 ensemble, with Sir Julien seated in the centre in the blazer.

Sir JULIEN CAHN'S CRICKET TEAM, 1937

Equipped throughout with "Viyella" Cricket Shirts, "Viyella" Socks.

Back Row, Left to Right

R. C. Butterworth
S. D. Rhodes
C. C. Goodway
J. B. Hall
R. J. Crisp
G. F. Summers
C. R. Maxwell

Front Row, Left to Right

J. Walsh
E. G. Wolfe
B. H Lyon
Sir Julien Cahn
D. P. B. Morkel
I. A. R. Peebles
C. S. Dempster

Seated on Ground

T. B. Reddick
H. Mudge

220. Bedfordshire Cricket XI, 1906. Edwardian elegance and casualness, with a mixture of straw boaters, blazers, and caps. Card published by F. Thurston of Luton.

221. Heathercliffe XI on their pavilion steps.

222. Ventnor 2nd XI, 1914.

223. A select Buckinghamshire XI at Bletchley Park in 1905.

224. Sandiacre Cricket Club (Nottinghamshire) proudly displaying a 1904 Championship trophy. All the players on this postcard by local publisher J. Marrin are identified, a rare event on this type of card.

225. E. 'Patsy' Hendren (1889-1962), Middlesex and England. In a career from 1907 to 1937 he scored 57,611 runs, with 151 centuries, and appeared in 51 Test matches. He was a much-loved cricketer wherever he played, and as a professional footballer performed for several clubs, including Manchester City and Brentford. Card published anonymously.

226. The third Test of the 1926 season was drawn after England followed on. They were saved by a Hobbs and Sutcliffe opening partnership of 156 - and rain. Jack Webb of Nottingham published the card.

227. G. Geary (1893-1981), Leicestershire and England. This fine and most popular all-rounder is seen on a card produced by the *Sport and General* newspaper. From 1912-38 (during which time he played in fourteen Test matches), Geary scored over 13,000 runs and took 2,063 wickets, averaging 20.93.

228. Arthur Mitchell (1902-1976), Yorkshire and England. Between 1922 and 1945 this Yorkshireman scored 18,034 runs for his county with true native grit and determination. Though he played in six Tests, he did not do himself justice, scoring only 298 runs (average 29.80). Mitchell went on to become Yorkshire county coach.

229. Tommy Worthington (1905-1973), Derbyshire and England. Worthington played for his county from 1924 to 1947, during which time he scored 17,000 runs and took 624 wickets. In nine Test matches he hit one century and totalled 321 runs.

AUSTRALIAN TEST TEAM - D. J. (DON) BRADMAN.

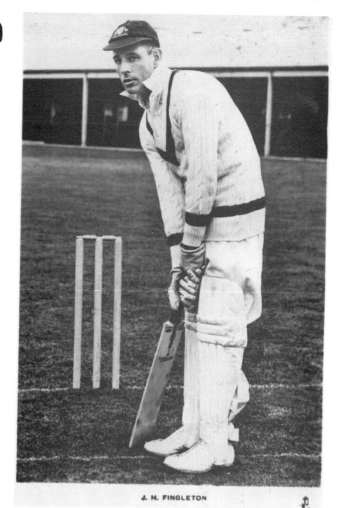

J. H. FINGLETON

230. Don Bradman (1908-   ), New South Wales, South Australia and Australia, scored 118 on his debut for N.S.W., and from then on for another 21 years (apart from the second world war) was the scourge of all bowlers he faced. In all he scored 28,067 runs (averaging 95.14) with a highest score of 452 not out (against Queensland in 1929-30). Postcard published anonymously, one of a series of the 1930 tourists to England.

231. Jack Fingleton (1908-1981), New South Wales and Australia. Not only a fine cricketer, but a radio commentator and author of the highest order. In a first-class career from 1930-40, he scored 6,816 runs. Card published by Raphael Tuck and Sons.

AUSTRALIAN TEST TEAM - C. W. WALKER.

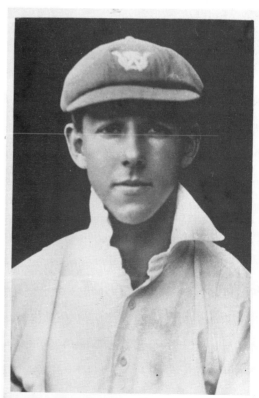

AUSTRALIAN TEST TEAM - A. JACKSON.

232. Charlie Walker (1909-1942), South Australia. Played for his state team from 1928-9 until the war, touring England twice, firstly as deputy to Oldfield (1930) and then Barnett (1938). He was killed in action over Germany in 1942.

233. Archie Jackson (1909-1933), New South Wales and Australia. Ill-health robbed the world of this brilliant batsman who in his short career thrilled all who saw him with his grace and elegance. He played in eight Test matches for Australia.

234. A scene at Edgbaston. Photographic card published about 1910 by Adams and Co., Birmingham.

235. T.W.S. Wiles, 33 George St., Hove, published this photographic card showing Vine going in to bat "for the first time this season" on 11th May 1914. A selection of Hove members perch on the rather primitive seating beside the pavilion, with a variety of headgear in evidence.

236. Trent Bridge on a 1929 postcard published by C. and A.G. Lewis of Nottingham, no. 3751 in their extensive series. Message reads: *"Just on my way to cricket match at Trent Bridge. Nice day ..... P.S. Just had an hour's priceless cricket! Derbyshire scoring 100 per hour!! Going straight back."* Posted on August 12th, 1929.